Edgar Thurston

Amphibia Southern India

Edgar Thurston

Amphibia Southern India

ISBN/EAN: 9783743332706

Manufactured in Europe, USA, Canada, Australia, Japa

Cover: Foto ©ninafisch / pixelio.de

Manufactured and distributed by brebook publishing software
(www.brebook.com)

Edgar Thurston

Amphibia Southern India

PREFACE.

The present Catalogue of the Batrachians of Southern India is the offspring of the Catalogues of the 'Batrachia Salientia S. Ecaudata' (1882) and 'Batrachia Gradientia S. Caudata and Batrachia Apoda' (1882), in the collection of the British Museum, by M. Boulenger, which I have followed throughout, and from which I have received more assistance than I can adequately express. I am further indebted to M. Boulenger for the identification of specimens which I sent to him at the British Museum.

Our knowledge of the rarer species of the Batrachians, which inhabit our Presidency, is mainly derived from the field labours of the late Mr. Jerdon and Colonel Beddome, by whom the majority of the specimens in the British Museum were presented.

Though as many as fifty-eight different species of Batrachians have been already recorded from Southern India, it is highly probable that some new species still remain to be discovered in the as yet imperfectly explored hill-ranges and forests; and of many which are already known, in some cases only from single specimens, much remains to be learnt as to their haunts, habits, and life-history.

It is worthy of notice that a large number of species are recorded in the British Museum Catalogue from Madras, but it is probable that, in some cases, the word Madras must refer to the Presidency and not to the city, for, so far as I know from personal observation, only the following species are found in, or in the vicinity of Madras itself, viz.: *Rana hexadactyla, Rana tigrina* (bull frog), *Rhacophorus maculatus* ('chunam frog'), *Microhyla rubra, Callula olivacea, Bufo melanostictus* (house toad), and *Cacopus systoma.*

EDGAR THURSTON,
Government Central Museum.

MADRAS,
July 1, 1888.

GENERAL NOTES.

THE Batrachia are placed, according to Huxley's system of classifica-
tion, with the Fishes (*Pisces*) among the ICHTHYOPSIDA, one of the three
groups [1] of Vertebrata.

They may be defined as cold-blooded (poikilothermic) vertebrate
animals, the majority of which have a pair of lungs situated below
the digestive tract, which breathe by means of gills during some or
the entire period of their existence, have three chambers (two auricles
and a ventricle) to the heart, and two or no occipital condyles. Their
limbs, if present, have not more than five fingers developed, and if, as is
rare, they possess dorsal fins, these are merely folds of the integuments
without those supporting cartilaginous rays which are found in fishes.

Recent Batrachians belong to the three following orders :—

1. *Ecaudata, Anura,* or tailless Batrachians ;
2. *Caudata,*[2] *Urodela,* or tailed Batrachians ;
3. *Apoda, Gymnophiona,* limbless Batrachians or Cœcilians.

Of these three orders, only two, the *Ecaudata* and *Apoda*, have been
recorded from Southern India, the former including the frogs and
toads, and the latter the worm-like Cœcilians.

The skin of Batrachians is, as a rule, naked, though the Cœcilians
have thick cutaneous rings, imbedded in which are small scales. The
cutaneous glands of many Batrachians secrete an acrid milky juice,
which not only serves to keep the skin moist, but also acts as an
irritant,[3] and serves as a means of self-defence. In some Batrachians,
e.g., the common South Indian toad (*Bufo melanostictus*), the glands
on the side of the neck form two prominent masses, and are called
the parotoids. In addition to its secretory function, the skin, which
is provided with an abundant blood-supply, is also an important
accessory organ of respiration, and it has been shown by experiment
that a frog can live for a long time after extirpation of its lungs by
means of its cutaneous respiration. In some Batrachians the highly
vascular swimming tail, lying against the egg-membrane, may serve
as a larval respiratory organ.

In most of the Batrachians the ova are impregnated and hatched
outside the body, and the young undergo a series of metamorphoses.
These changes or metamorphoses are partially represented as they occur

---

[1] ICHTHYOPSIDA, SAUROPSIDA (*Reptilia* and *Aves*), and MAMMALIA.

[2] Writing concerning the geographical distribution of the Batrachia in the Indian
region, Boulenger says : "Two forms of *Caudata* occur, viz., *Tylotriton*, in Yunnan and
the Himalayas, and a species of the otherwise entirely North American genus *Amblystoma*,
which has been found in the mountains of Laos. These forms, however, cannot be
considered to be characteristic of the Indian region, but should be regarded as immigrants
from the northern zone ; and, in fact, they seem to be limited to such altitudes as compen-
sate the difference of latitude." Cat. Batr. Grad., 1882, p. 412.

[3] Handling the common English toad is said to be frequently succeeded by inflam-
mation of the eye-lid.

in the larva or tadpole of one of the South Indian frogs (fig. 1), which, when hatched, has a long compressed tail, and breathes by means of

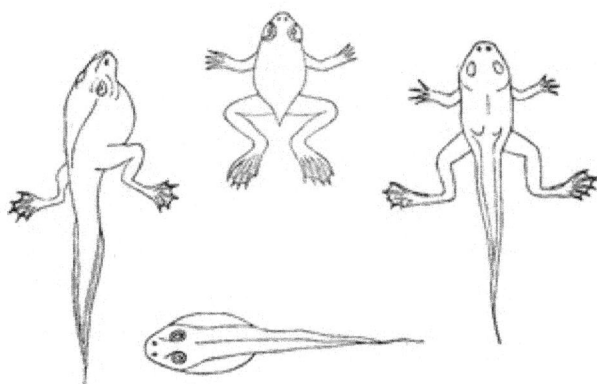

Fig. 1.

external gills. As development advances, the lung sacs take on functional activity, and the posterior extremities make their appearance, being followed later on by the anterior extremities, which have meanwhile been hidden and developing beneath the skin. The tadpole, which is now a four-legged air-breathing animal, has only to lose its swimming tail to assume its perfect form and become adapted for a terrestrial as well as an aquatic life.

"The alimentary canal of the tadpole is at first long and coiled up in a close spire, like a watch-spring, in the abdomen, but its length becomes relatively less as age advances. At the same time, the diet changes from vegetable to animal, the young tadpole being chiefly herbivorous, the adult insectivorous." (Huxley.)

The males of many species of Batrachian, *e.g.*, the South Indian bull frog (*Rana tigrina*) and *Cacopus systoma* (pl. ix) have a single sac or a pair of sacs on the throat, called the sub-gular vocal sacs, which open into the mouth cavity, and act as resonants to the waves of sound set up by the air which is passing from the lungs, and help to increase the intensity of the familiar Batrachian chorus by intensifying the sound produced by the vocal cords.

In his observations on sexual differences between the males and females of Batrachian species, Darwin says [1] :—" With respect to sexual differences of colour, Dr. Günther does not know of any striking instance either with frogs or toads, yet he can often distinguish the male from the female by the tints of the former being a little more intense. Nor does he know of any striking difference in external structure between the sexes, excepting the prominences which become developed during the breeding season on the front legs of the male, by which he is

[1] The Descent of Man, 2nd ed., 1875, p. 349.

enabled to hold the female.[1] It is surprising that these animals have not acquired more strongly-marked sexual characters, for, though cold-blooded, their passions are strong. Dr. Günther informs me that he has several times found an unfortunate female toad dead and smothered from having been so closely embraced by three or four males. Frogs have been observed by Professor Hoffman in Giessen fighting all day long during the breeding season, and with so much violence that one had its body ripped open.

" Frogs and toads offer one interesting sexual difference, namely, in the musical powers possessed by the males ; but to speak of music, when applied to the discordant and overwhelming sounds emitted by male bull-frogs and some other species, seems, according to our taste, a singularly inappropriate expression. Nevertheless, certain frogs sing in a decidedly pleasing manner. [2] Near Rio Janeiro I used often to sit in the evening to listen to a number of little Hylæ, perched on blades of grass close to the water, which sent forth sweet chirping notes in harmony. The various sounds are emitted chiefly by the males during the breeding season, as in the case of the croaking of our common frog. " In accordance with this fact the vocal organs of the males are more highly developed than those of the females. In some genera the males alone are provided with sacs which open into the larynx. For instance in the edible frog (*Rana esculenta*) the sacs are peculiar to the males, and become, when filled with air in the act of croaking, large globular bladders, standing out one on each side of the head near the corners of the mouth. The croak of the male is thus rendered exceedingly powerful, whilst that of the female is only a slight groaning noise."

In some Batrachians, *e.g.*, the American *Pipa*, there is no tongue, but all the South Indian tailless Batrachians possess a tongue, which is attached in a different manner to that of the higher vertebrata, being fixed in front between the rami of the lower jaw (*Opisthoglossa*) and frequently bifid or emarginate and free behind and capable of being projected out of the mouth (fig. 2), and acting as an organ of prehension.

Fig. 2.

In some species, *e.g.*, *Rana diplosticta* (pl. V, fig. 3), the tongue has a free conical prominence called the papilla on the middle of its upper surface.

---

[1] Dr. J. Anderson has described the sexual characters of the male of *Bufo sikkimensis*, Blyth, as consisting of "two plate-like callosities on each side of the thorax, thickly studded with minute dark-brown granules, such as occur on the same region in *B. liebigi* and other Batrachia. Similar to these structures is the rough, almost spiny surface on the upper aspect of the first and second fingers and on the inner margin of the third. The female, as in other Batrachia, has no trace of these structures." *Proc. Zool. Soc.*, 1871, p. 204.

[2] The male of the South Indian toad, *Bufo melanostictus*, occasionally emits a clear, sharp musical note, which is not at all unpleasant.

The tailless Batrachians of Southern India, which, in common with those from other regions, have the posterior extremities considerably longer than the anterior, belong to the three following families :—

1. The *Ranidæ*, or true frogs ;
2. The *Engystomatidæ* ;
3. The *Bufonidæ*, or true toads.

The *Ranidæ*, represented in Southern India by the genera *Rana, Rhacophorus, Ixalus, Nyctibatrachus,* and *Nannobatrachus,* have their pectoral arch or girdle constructed on the "Firmisternal" type (*r.p.* 9), possess teeth in their upper jaw, and the transverse processes of their sacral vertebra are not or only very slightly dilated (pl. I, fig. 4. sv.).

Fig. 3.

Some genera, *e.g.,* *Rana,* have the fingers perfectly free, and the toes more or less completely webbed (fig. 3), while other genera, *e.g.,* *Rhacophorus,* have the fingers as well as the toes more or less webbed. The feet of many of the *Ranidæ* are provided with one or more metatarsal tubercles (fig. 4), which

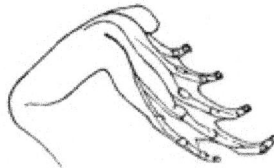

Fig. 4.

may be blunt, sharp, or, *e.g.,* in *Rana breviceps,* shovel-shaped and well-adapted for digging.

Many of the *Ranidæ* lead an arboreal life, and some, *e.g.,* the common "chunam frog" (*Rhacophorus maculatus*), have well-developed discs at the ends of their fingers and toes (fig. 5), by means of which they are able to stick on to smooth vertical surfaces, such as walls and windows.

Fig. 5.

Taking as a type of the bony skeleton of the *Ranidæ* the skeleton (pls. I and II) of *Rana hexadactyla,* a species which is very common in tanks and along river banks throughout Southern India, its leading features are as follows :—

1. The bony skull is large and flattened. On the superior surface (pl. I, 1) may be recognised a large *fronto-parietal* (*fp*) formed by the union

of the *frontal* and *parietal* bones, and articulating anteriorly with the united *nasals* (*n*); on each side of the *fronto-parietal* and intervening between it and the *squamosal*, the *pro-otic* (*po*). The *squamosals* (*sq*) articulate with the *quadrato-jugals* (*qj*), in front of which are the tooth-bearing *maxilla* (*m*) and *præmaxillæ* (*pm*).

On the inferior surface (pl. I, 2) are the *vomers* (*vo*) with the vomerine teeth arranged in two oblique series, the transverse *palatines* (*pl*), *spheneth-moid* (*s*), *parasphenoid* (*psp*), and the *pterygoids* (*pt*). On the posterior surface are the large *exoccipitals* (*eo*), which articulate with the first vertebra or *atlas* [1] by means of two condyles, one on either side of the *foramen magnum*. The *inferior maxillæ* (pl. I, 3) are made up of several bones and connected together at the symphysis by a *symphyseal* bone (*sy*).

2. The vertebral column (pl. I, 4) is made up of eight *præsacral* vertebræ, one *sacral* vertebra (*sv*) and a long modified caudal portion called the *urostyle* (*c*), which articulates with the convex articular surfaces of the *sacral* vertebra by two corresponding concave surfaces. All the vertebræ, except the first or *atlas*, have transverse processes.

3. The pelvic girdle (pl. I, 5) is composed of two long narrow ilia (*il*), which are connected anteriorly with the *sacral* vertebræ and posteriorly with the *pubis* and *ischium* (*pi*), which, in this species, are completely fused together, so that the bottom of the cavity of the *acetabulum*, which receives the head of the *femur*, is traversed by a transverse fissure instead of a triradiate fissure, such as is formed in the European *Rana esculenta* by the junction of the ilium, ischium, and pubis.

4. The posterior extremity (pl. II, 1, 2, 3) is made up of the *femur* (*f*), the united *tibia* and *fibula* (*tf*), the *tarsus* (*ca*), in which the *calcaneum* and *astragalus* (*tibiale* and *fibulare*) appear as two long bones united at their proximal and distal extremities, the *metatarsus* (*mts*) and *phalanges* (*ph*). The toes are five in number, and there is in addition on the inner side of the base of the metatarsal bone of the first toe or *hallux*, a small bone called the *calcar* (*c*), which may be considered as a rudimentary sixth toe.

5. In the pectoral arch or girdle (pl. II, 4) the following parts can be recognised:—The *scapula* (*sc*) with the cartilaginous *supra scapula* (*ssc*), *precoracoid* (*pc*), and *coracoid* (*co*), of which the latter is connected with its fellow of the opposite side in the middle line. Batrachians which have the *coracoids* thus connected are placed in the "Firmisternal" series to distinguish them from those Batrachians, *e.g.*, the South Indian toad (*Bufo melanostictus*), which belong to the "Arciferous" series, in which the *precoracoid* and *coracoid* are connected by an arciform cartilage, which overlaps the corresponding cartilage of the opposite side (fig. 6). Anterior to, and articulating with, the internal extremities of the *precoracoids* is the partly cartilaginous and partly osseous *omosternum* (*ost*), and posterior to and articulating with the *coracoids* is the ossified *sternum* (*st*), with its attached

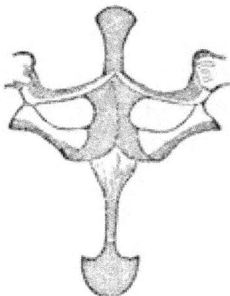

Fig. 6.

[1] "In amphibians the first vertebra consists of a simple ring, which articulates with the two condyles and the basis cranii. As numerous researches have shown, however, the first vertebra of amphibians does not correspond to that (*i.e.*, the atlas) of the higher vertebrates, but is much more nearly homologous with the second cervical vertebra of the latter, the axis." *Wiedersheim, Comparative Anatomy of Vertebrates*, (Engl. Transl.), 1886.

xiphisternum (*xst*), the latter being like the *omosternum* only partly ossified. The *glenoid cavity*, which receives the head of the *humerus* is formed by the *coracoid, præcoracoid,* and *scapula.*

6. The anterior extremity (pl. II, 5) is made up of the *humerus* (*h*), *radius* and *ulna* (*rul*), which are fused into a single bone, *carpus* (*cp*), *metacarpus* (*mcp*), and *phalanges* (*ph*). The functional digits of the manus are four in number, but there is, in addition, a very rudimentary representative of a thumb or *pollex,* corresponding to the *hallux* of the pes.

The *Engystomidæ,* which, like the Ranidæ, belong to the "Firmisternal" series, but have no maxillary teeth and have the transverse processes of the sacral vertebra dilated, are represented in Southern India by the genera *Melanobatrachus,* of which only one species (*M. indicus*), recorded by Colonel Beddome from the Anamallays, is known, *Microhyla, Callula,* and *Cacopus,* of which the last named contains the unsightly *Cacopus globulosus.* "This family," Boulenger writes,[1] "includes terrestrial, aquatic and burrowing types, but no arboreal—*Callula, Brachymerus,* and others generally regarded as 'tree frogs,' being merely aquatic or terrestrial in spite of their digital dilatations. For the purpose of burrowing, either the hind pair of limbs (*Hypopachus, Glyphoglossus, Cacopus, Breviceps, &c.*), or the front pair (*Hemisus*) are particularly strengthened and provided with a corneous sheath.

In the last-named genera, the mouth is very narrow, and those frogs may be considered "ant-eaters," similarly as the bufonid genus "*Rhinophrynus.*"

The specimen of *Cacopus globulosus* in the Madras Museum, which was captured at Russellkonda, has its stomach distended with an enormous mass of winged "white ants."

The *Bufonidæ* belong to the "Arciferous" series (*v.p.* 9), and, like the *Engystomidæ,* have no maxillary teeth, and the transverse processes or diapophyses of the sacral vertebra are dilated. They are represented in Southern India by a single species of *Nectophryne* and by several species of *Bufo,* of which the most common is the familiar house toad (*Bufo melanostictus*), concerning which Sir J. Emerson Tennent writes[2] :—
"The belief in its venomous nature is as old as the third century B.C., when the *Mahawanso* mentions that the wife of King Asoka attempted to destroy the great Bo tree at Magadha with the poisoned fang of a toad."

The limbless Batrachians (*Apoda*), of which the males have an intromittent copulatory organ consisting of the eversible cloaca which is regulated by well-developed muscles, are represented in Southern India by two genera, *Ichthyophis* and *Uræotyphlus,* long worm-like burrowing animals, which belong to the family Cœciliidæ. "In these Batrachians," says Günther,[3] "a tail is absent or extremely short. The skin is smooth and viscous, forming numerous annular folds; transverse series of rudimentary scales are imbedded in these folds, especially in those of the posterior part of the body.

"Their eyes are rudimentary, more or less hidden below the skin.

"They constantly live below ground, burrowing like worms; their food appears to consist of mould and worms. The metamorphosis is less complete than in the two previous orders (tailless and tailed Batra-

[1] Cat. Bir. sal. 1882, p. 147.   [2] Ceylon. 1860, vol. I, p. 202.
[3] Rept. Brit. Ind. 1864, p. 440.

chians) ; the young do not live in the water, and have quite the external appearance of the old ones, but they are provided with short gills, which do not project from the gill-openings. Gills and gill-openings disappear at an early period, and the perfect animal has only one lung developed, the other remaining rudimentary as in most snakes."

The Cœcilians possess a remarkable organ, the so-called " tentacle," which is closely related as regards its position both to the nasal cavity and to the orbit, and concerning which Wiedersheim says (op. cit). " The physiological function of this apparatus, which occurs quite isolated in the animal kingdom, cannot at present be explained with certainty. It probably acts as a spouting apparatus, and (if the secretions of the glands be poisonous) as a weapon of offence, and thus, together with the remarkably developed olfactory organ, it would serve in some measure to make up for the non-functional, or partly non-functional, eyes and auditory organ. It is improbable that it serves as a " tentacle," or organ of touch, as was formerly supposed, as the necessary nerves and sensory epithelium are not known to be present."

Table showing the Proportions of the known Genera and Species of South Indian Batrachians.

ECAUDATA.

FIRMISTERNIA.

RANIDÆ.

	Number of species.
Rana	17
Rhacophorus	5
Ixalus	14
Nyctibatrachus	2
Nannobatrachus	1

ENGYSTOMATIDÆ.

Melanobatrachus	1
Microhyla	2
Callula	3
Cacopus	2

ARCIFERA.

BUFONIDÆ.

Nectophryne	1
Bufo	6

APODA.

CŒCILIIDÆ.

Ichthyophis	2
Uræotyphlus	2
Total	48

List of the Batrachians of the Nilgiris.[1]

BATRACHIA ECAUDATA.

RANIDÆ.

Rana beddomii, *Günth.*	Walaghát.
,, breviceps, *Schn.*	Slopes
,, curtipes, *Jerd.*	Walaghát and the Ouchterlony valley.
,, cyanophlyctis. *Schn.*	Eastern slopes.
,, diplosticta, *Günth.*	Walaghát.
,, gracilis, *Wiegm.*	Plateau. The common frog in the swamps.
,, hexadactyla, *Less.*	Eastern slopes.
,, kuhlii, *Schleg.*	Walaghát.
,, temporalis, *Günth.*	Plateau and slopes.
,, tigrina, *Daud.*	Eastern slopes and plateau.
,, verrucosa, *Günth.*	Western slopes.
Rhacophorus maculatus, *Gray.*	Lower slopes.
,, pleurostictus, *Günth.*	Ootacamund and all the plateau.
Ixalus glandulosus, *Jerd.*	Plateau and slopes.
,, opisthorhodus, *Günth.*	Plateau and slopes.
,, saxicola, *Jerd.*	Western slopes, on rocks, beds of rivers, &c.
,, signatus, *Blga.*	Pycara and Eastern slopes.
,, variabilis, *Günth.*	Plateau and slopes.
Nyctibatrachus pygmæus, *Günth.*	Walaghát.

ENGYSTOMATIDÆ.

Melanobatrachus indicus, *Bedd.*	Walaghát.
Microhyla ornata, *D. & B.*	Eastern slopes.
,, rubra, *Jerd.*	Walaghát, &c.
Callula obscura, *Günth.*	Plateau, western side and slopes.
,, olivacea, *Günth.*	Walaghát.
,, picta, *Bibr.*	Slopes near Gajalhatti.
,, triangularis, *Günth.*	Pycara and Kótagiri.
Cacopus systoma, *Schn.*	Slopes.

BUFONIDÆ.

Bufo beddomii, *Günth.*	Western slopes.
,, hololius, *Günth.*	Do.
,, melanostictus, *Schn.*	Common everywhere.
,, microtympanum *Blga.*	Coonoor.

APODA.

CŒCILIIDÆ

Ichthyophis glutinosus. *L.*	Western slopes.
Uræotyphlus oxyurus, *D & B.*	Do.

[1] This list is based on Colonel Beddome's List of the Frogs of the Nilgiris in the "Manual of the Nilagiri District," (1880). I have omitted a species which is there recorded as " Crinia (or allied genus) n.sp." and described as " a minute frog with free toes. No parotids. maxillary teeth, and sacral vertebræ sometimes dilated ; " found at Walaghát.

Table showing the Batrachians recorded from South India and Ceylon.[1]

	South India.	Ceylon.
ORDER I.—ECAUDATA.		
FAMILY.—RANIDÆ.		
1. Rana, *Linn.*		
1. hexadactyla, *Less.*	*	*
2. cyanophlyctis, *Schn.*	*	*
3. corrugata, *Ptrs.*	*	*
4. tigrina, *Daud.*	*	*
5. kuhlii, *Schleg.*	*	*
6. gracilis, *Wiegm.*	*	*
7. verrucosa, *Günth.*	*	
8. rufescens, *Jerd.*	*	
9. breviceps, *Schn.*	*	*
10. dobsonii, *Blgr.*	*	
11. beddomii, *Günth.*	*	
12. semipalmata, *Blgr.*	*	
13. leptodactyla, *Blgr.*	*	
14. diplosticta, *Günth.*	*	
15. phrynoderma, *Blgr.*	*	
16. malabarica, *Bibr.*	*	
17. curtipes, *Jerd.*	*	
18. macularia, *Blyth.*	*	*
19. temporalis, *Günth.*	*	*
2. Rhacophorus, *Kuhl.*		
1. pleurostictus, *Günth.*	*	
2. stictomerus, *Günth.*		*
3. microtympanum, *Günth.*		*
4. reticulatus, *Günth.*		*
5. nanus, *Günth.*		*
6. fergusonii, *Blgr.*		*
7. cavirostris, *Günth.*		*
8. maculatus, *Gray.*		
9. malabaricus, *Jerd.*	*	
10. beddomii, *Blgr.*	*	
11. eques, *Günth.*		*
12. nasutus, *Günth.*		*
13. ————— ?		*
14. lateralis, *Blgr.*	*	
3. Ixalus, *D. & Bibr.*		
1. opisthorhodus, *Günth.*	*	
2. fuscus, *Blgr.*	*	
3. silvaticus, *Blgr.*	*	
4. saxicola, *Jerd.*	*	

[1] See First Report on the Collection of Batrachia in the Colombo Museum, by A. Haly, Director.

It must be borne in mind that a great part of the Madras Presidency is placed by Wallace in the same sub-region (the Ceylonese) of the Oriental region as the island of Ceylon. Concerning the amphibia of this sub-region, Wallace says (*Geograph. Distribution of Animals*, 1876, vol. 1, 327), "The genera of amphibians that occur here are generally of wide range, but *Nannophys*, *Haplobatrachus*, and *Cacopus* are confined to the sub-region, while *Megalophys* is Malayan, and the species found in Ceylon also inhabit Java."

Table showing the Batrachians, &c.—continued.

—	South India.	Ceylon.
ORDER I.—ECAUDATA—*continued.*		
FAMILY.—RANIDÆ—*continued.*		
3. Ixalus, *D. and Bibr.*—continued.		
5. hypomelas, *Günth.*		*
6. oxyrhyncus, *Günth.*		*
7. leucorhinus, *Mart.*	*	*
8. schmardanus, *Kelaart.*		*
9. nasutus, *Günth.*		*
10. femoralis, *Günth.*	*	*
11. bedomii, *Günth.*	*	
12. pulcher, *Blgr.*	*	
13. variabilis, *Günth.*	*	*
14. adspersus, *Günth.*		*
15. glandulosus, *Jerd.*	*	
16. punctatus, *And.*	*	
17. chalazodes, *Günth.*	*	
18. flaviventris, *Blgr.*	*	
19. signatus, *Blgr.*	*	
4. Nyctibatrachus, *Blgr.*		
1. pygmæus, *Günth.*	*	
2. major, *Blgr.*	*	
5. Nannobatrachus, *Blgr.*		
1. beddomii, *Blgr.*	*	
6. Nannophrys, *Günth.*		
1. ceylonensis, *Günth*		*
2. guentheri, *Blgr.*		*
FAMILY.—ENGYSTOMATIDÆ.		
1. Melanobatrachus, *Blgr.*		
1. indicus, *Bedd.*	*	
2. Microhyla, *Tsch.*		
1. rubra, *Jerd.*	*	*
2. ornata, *D. & Bibr.*	*	
3. Callula, *Gray*		
1. obscura, *Günth.*	*	*
2. olivacea, *Günth.*	*	
3. triangularis, *Günth.*	*	
4. pulchra, *Gray*		*
4. Cacopus, *Günth.*		
1. systoma, *Schn.*	*	*
2. globulosus, *Günth.*	*	
FAMILY.—BUFONIDÆ.		
1. Nectophryne, *Buch. & Ptrs.*		
1. tuberculosa, *Günth.*	*	
2. Bufo, *Laur.*		
1. pulcher, *Blgr.*	*	

Table showing the Batrachians, &c.—continued.

—	South India.	Ceylon.
ORDER I.—ECAUDATA—*continued.*		
FAMILY.—BUFONIDÆ—*continued.*		
2. Bufo, *Laur*—continued.		
2. hololius, *Gunth.*	*	
3. beddomii, *Gunth.*	*	
4. melanostictus, *Schn.*	*	*
5. microtympanum, *Blgr.*	*	
6. parietalis, *Blgr.*	*	*
7. kelaartii, *Gunth.*		*
FAMILY.—PELOBATIDÆ.		
1. Megalophrys, *Kuhl.*		
1. montana, *Kuhl.*		*
ORDER II.—APODA.		
FAMILY.—CŒCILIIDÆ.		
1. Ichthyophis, *Fitz.*		
1. glutinosus, *L.*	*	*
2. monochrous, *Blgr.*	*	
2. Uræotyphlus, *Ptrs.*		
1. oxyurus, *D. & Bibr.*	*	
2. malabaricus, *Bedd.*	*	

SYSTEMATIC INDEX.

CLASS.—BATRACHIA.

ORDER I.—ECAUDATA.

SUB-ORDER I.—PHANEROGLOSSA.

SERIES A.—FIRMISTERNIA.

FAMILY 1.—RANIDÆ.

CATALOGUE

OF

SOUTH INDIAN BATRACHIA.

BATRACHIA.

ORDER I.—ECAUDATA.

In the perfect state, four limbs and no tail.

SUB-ORDER 1.—PHANEROGLOSSA.

Eustachian tubes separated; a tongue.

Series A.—FIRMISTERNIA.

Coracoids firmly united by a simple epicoracoid cartilage; precoracoids, if present, resting with their distal extremity upon the coracoids, or connected with the latter by the epicoracoid cartilage.

FAMILY 1.—RANIDÆ.

Upper jaw toothed; diapophyses of sacral vertebra cylindrical, or very slightly dilated.   p. 20.

FAMILY 2.—ENGYSTOMATIDÆ.

Maxillary teeth none; diapophyses of sacral vertebra dilated. p. 40.

Series B.—ARCIFERA.

Coracoids and precoracoids connected by an arched cartilage, that of the one side overlapping that of the other.

FAMILY 3.—BUFONIDÆ.

Maxillary teeth none; diapophyses of sacral vertebra dilated. p. 44.

1. RANIDÆ.

Upper jaw toothed; diapophyses of sacral vertebra not, or only very slightly, dilated.

Synopsis of Genera.

Pupil horizontal; tongue more or less deeply emarginate; vomerine teeth; fingers perfectly free, toes webbed; outer metatarsals separated by web; omosternum and sternum with a bony style.

1. Rana, p. 20.

Characters of *Rana*, but the fingers more or less webbed.

2. Rhacophorus, p. 29.

Pupil horizontal; tongue deeply emarginate; vomerine teeth none; outer metatarsals separated by a groove or narrow web; omosternum and sternum with a bony style. 3. Ixalus, p. 33.

Pupil vertical; tongue deeply emarginate; vomerine teeth; toes webbed; outer metatarsals separated by a web; omosternum and sternum with a bony style.

4. Nyctibatrachus, p. 39.

Pupil vertical; tongue rather deeply emarginate; vomerine teeth; toes free; outer metatarsals separated by a groove; omosternum and sternum slender, cartilaginous. 5. Nannobatrachus, p. 39.

1. RANA.

Synopsis of Species.

A. *Fingers and toes acutely pointed, the latter very broadly webbed.*

First finger extending a little beyond second.

1. *hexadactyla*, p. 21.

First finger not extending beyond second.

2. *cyanophlyctis*, p. 22.

B. *Finger pointed or blunt; toes blunt or slightly dilated at the tips.*

1. Toes more than half webbed.

a. Tympanum hidden, first finger extending a little beyond second; upper eyelid rather narrow. 3. *kuhlii*, p. 22.

b. Tympanum perfectly distinct.

A much developed membranaceous fringe along the outer side of the fifth toe; interorbital space narrower than the upper eyelid.

4. *tigrina*, p. 23.

Tibio-tarsal articulation reaching the tip of the snout[1]; upper parts strongly warty. 5. *verrucosa*, p. 25.

2. Toes not more than half webbed.

Inner metatarsal tubercle blunt. 6. *gracilis*, p. 24.

Inner metatarsal tubercle shovel-shaped; tarso-metatarsal articulation reaching a little beyond the tip of the snout.

7. *rufescens*, p. 25.

Inner metatarsal tubercle shovel-shaped; tympanum two-thirds the size of the eye. 8. *dobsonii*, p. 26.

Inner metatarsal tubercle shovel-shaped; tympanum half the size of the eye. 9. *breviceps*, p. 25.

---

[1] This measurement is estimated by drawing the hind limb forwards.

C. *Tips of fingers and toes more or less dilated.*

1. A glandular lateral fold.

a. Tips of fingers and toes simply swollen.

Toes half webbed ; tibio-tarsal articulation reaching the eye.
10. *malabarica,* p. 28.

Toes nearly entirely webbed; tibio-tarsal articulation reaching the eye; head large. 11. *curtipes,* p. 28.

b. Tips of fingers and toes dilated into regular discs; vomerine teeth extending beyond the level of the hinder edge of the choanæ.

Interorbital space as broad as the upper eyelid; tympanum three-fourths the size of the eye. 12. *temporalis,* p. 29.

2. No glandular lateral fold.

a. Vomerine teeth not extending beyond the level of the hinder edge of the choanæ.

Upper surface very warty ; toes one-fourth webbed.
13. *phrynoderma,* p. 27.

b. Vomerine teeth extending beyond the level of the hinder edge of the choanæ; a free conical papilla on the middle of the tongue; discs of fingers and toes small.

Toes two-thirds webbed. 14. *beddomii,* p. 26.

Toes half webbed. 15. *semipalmata,* p. 27.

Toes one-third webbed. 16. *leptodactyla,* p. 27.

Toes one-third webbed ; a black spot on the loin.
17. *diplosticta,* p. 27.

1. RANA HEXADACTYLA [PLATE III].

Rana hexadactyla, *Lesson in Bélang. Voy. Ind. Or. Rept.* p. 331 ; *Tschudi, Batr.* p. 80; *Steindachn Novara. Amph.* p. 19; *Günth. Cat.* 1858, p. 11, and *Rept. Brit. Ind.* 1864, p. 405, and *Proc. Zool. Soc.* 1875, p. 568 ; *Blgr. Cat.* 1882, p. 17.

Dactylethra bengalensis. *Lesson, Ill. Zool.* pl. 47.

Rana cutipora, *Dum. & Bibr.* p. 339 ; *Jerdon, Journ. As. Soc. Beng.* 1853, p. 531.

Rana robusta, *Blyth. Journ. As. Soc. Beng.* 1854, p. 298.

Skin smooth, with rows of pores round the neck, sides, and belly ; toes and fingers pointed, the first finger extending a little beyond the second ; toes webbed to the tips ; fourth toe not very much longer than third and fifth ; a membranaceous fringe along the margins of the first and fifth toes ; metatarsus with a single small inner conical tubercle. Colour generally bright grass-green, rapidly changing in spirit to chocolate brown, with a central green or yellow stripe (vertebral line) along the middle of the back, but the presence of this stripe is not constant.

This species is very common in tanks and along the banks of rivers throughout Southern India. Length of the body of the largest specimen in the Madras Museum, measured from the tip of the nose to the vent,

$3\frac{1}{16}$ inches; length of the hind leg, measured from the vent to the extremity of the longest toe, 4 inches.[1]

Specimens are recorded by Günther (*Rept. Brit. Ind.*) whose bodies attained to a length of $5\frac{1}{2}$ inches, the hind limb being 8 inches (measured from the vent).

As regards the utility of tank frogs to fishes, Mr. H. S. Thomas says :[2] "The frogs also, which have been existing on land the while, living on the insects with which India is rife, suddenly appear in multitudes on the filling of the tanks, and, unfriendly though they are to fry, make up for it by betaking themselves from the land to be food for fishes, notably for the *Ophiocephaleidæ* and *Siluridæ*."

2. RANA CYANOPHLYCTIS [PLATE IV. 1].   •

Rana cyanophlyctis, *Schneid. Hist. Amph.* 1. p. 137 ; *Peters, Mon. Berl. Ac.* 1863, p. 78 ; *Günth. Rept. Brit. Ind.* 1864, p. 406; *Steindachn, Novara. Amph.* p. 20; *Stoliczka, Proc. As. Soc. Beng.* 1872, p. 102 ; *Blgr. Cat.* 1882, p. 17.

Rana leschenhaultii, *Günth. Cat.* 1858, p. 11 ; *Dum. & Bibr.* p. 342 ; *Cantor. Cat. Mal. Rept.* p. 138.

Rana bengalensis, *Gray, Ind. Zool.* ; *Kelaart, Prodr. Faun. Zeyl.* 1852, p. 192.

Dicroglossus adolfi, *Günth. Proc. Zool. Soc.* 1860, p. 158, pl. 28, f. B, and *Rept. Brit. Ind.* 1864, p. 402.

Skin with small tubercles and warts above ; besides, more or less distinct rows of pores. Fingers and toes pointed, the first finger not extending beyond the second ; toes webbed to the tips, which are pointed ; fourth toe not much longer than the third and fifth ; inner metatarsal tubercle very like a rudimentary sixth toe. Colour and markings (of spirit specimens) : brown, or brownish olive above, dark spotted or marbled ; two blackish or brownish streaks on the hinder side of the thighs seldom absent ; beneath often speckled with blackish.

"This species" Günther says (*Rept. Brit. Ind.*) "is closely allied to *R. hexadactyla*, but remains much smaller, specimens from $1\frac{3}{4}$ to 2 inches long being fully mature ; the longest example I have examined is $2\frac{1}{2}$ inches long, the hind limb measuring $3\frac{3}{4}$ inches. It differs constantly from *R. hexadactyla* in having a longer thigh."

Specimens in the British Museum from the Nilgiris, Malabar, and Godávari valley ; in the Madras Museum from Madras : greatest length of body $1\frac{1}{2}$ inches; of hind leg $2\frac{3}{4}$ inches.

3. RANA KUHLII.

Rana kuhlii (*Schleg.*), *Dum. & Bibr.*, p. 384 ; *Anders. Anat. Zool. Res. Yunnan.* 1878, p. 838 ; *Blgr. Cat.* 1882, p. 20.

Rana kuhlii, part, *Gunth. Rept., Brit. Ind.* 1864. p. 404, pl. XXVI, f. A, and *Cat.* 1858, p. 8.

Rana conspicillata, *Günth. Proc. Zool. Soc.* 1872, p. 595, pl. 40, f. A ; *id. Zool. Record.* 1872, vol. IX, p. 79.

---

[1] In every case the length of the body is measured from the tip of the nose to the vent, and the length of the hind leg from the vent to the extremity of the longest toe.
[2] Tank Angling in India, 1887.

Upper surface with short longitudinal glandular folds or rounded tubercles, but sometimes smooth, except upon the tibiæ. Vomerine teeth in two small oblique series behind the choanæ; lower jaw with two more or less developed tooth-like prominences in front; tympanum hidden; eyes very prominent; fingers tapering; toes broadly webbed, the tips dilated into small discs; a narrow cutaneous fringe along the inner metatarsal edge, including a single long narrow tubercle. Colour and markings (of spirit specimens) : brown above with darker marbling; a reddish-brown transverse band with darker edges between the eyes; lower parts whitish, throat and inner side of the hind limbs marbled with brown.

Recorded by Colonel Beddome[1] from Walaghát (Nilgiris). Two specimens in the Madras Museum from the Nilgiris, which agree very closely with the young specimen from Ningpo, figured by Günther;[2] length of body 1¾ inches, hind leg 2¾ inches.

Concerning this species, Günther says (*l.c.*) : "This frog is not uncommon in Ceylon, and is found in Java, Celebes, and at Ningpo in China. The usual size of the specimens in European collections is not much more than 2 inches, but I have examined a specimen, the body of which is 4½ inches long, the hind limb measuring 6 inches."

4. RANA TIGRINA.

Rana tigrina, *Günth. Cat.* 1858, p. 9 ; *Daud. Rain.* p. 64, pl. XX, and *Rept.* VIII, p. 125 ; *Merr. Tent.* p. 174 ; *Cuv. R. A.; Dum. & Bib.* p. 375 ; *Kelaart. Prodr. Faun. Zeyl.* 1852, p. 192 ; *Peters, Mon. Berl. Ac.* 1863, p. 77 ; *Günth. Rept. Brit. Ind.* 1864, p. 407, and *Proc. Zool. Soc.* 1875, p. 567 ; *Steindachn, Novara. Amph.* p. 17 ; *Anderson, Anat. Zool. Res. Yunnan.* 1878. p. 837 ; *Blgr. Cat.* 1882, p. 26.

Rana cancrivora, (*Boie*) *Gravenh. Delic.* p. 41 ; *Tschudi, Batr.* p. 79.

Rana brama, *Lesson in Bélang, Voy. Ind. Or. Rept.* p. 329, pl. 6.

Rana vittigera, *Wiegm. Nova. Acta. Ac. Leop.* 1835, p. 225, t. 21. f. I.

Rana rugulosa, *Wiegm. l.c.* p. 258, t. 21. f. 2.

Rana crassa, *Jerdon, Journ. As. Soc. Beng.* 1853, p. 531; *Theobald, Cat. Rept. As. Soc. Mus.* p. 79 ; *Anderson. Proc. Zool. Soc.* 1871, p. 199.

Rana latrans, *David, Nouv. Arch. Mus.* VII, 1871, *Bull.* p. 76.

Rana mugiens, *Daud. Rain.* pl. XXIII ; *Latr. Rept.* Vol II, p. 153.

Hydrostentor pantherinus, *Fitzing. Sitz. Ac. Wien.* xlii. p. 414.

Pyxicephalus fodiens, *Peters, Mon. Berl. Ac.* 1860, p. 186.

Hoplobatrachus ceylanicus, *Peters, Mon. Berl. Ac.*, 1863, p. 449 ; *Günth. Rept. Brit. Ind.* 1864, p. 410.

Skin of the back with longitudinal folds ; tympanum distinct, about two-thirds the size of the eye ; lower jaw with two not very prominent apophyses in front ; fourth toe one-third or one-half longer than the fifth ; toes nearly entirely webbed, the web extending not quite to the tip of the fourth toe ; a well-developed membranaceous fringe along the outer side of the fifth toe ; a single small or large, blunt or shovel-shaped inner metatarsal tubercle. Colour dark-brown above with large

---

[1] Manual of the N lagiri District, 1880, p. 175.
[2] Rept., Brit. Ind., pl. XXVI B.

blackish spots. Frequently a light vertebral line running from the nose to the vent. Anderson says (*l.c.*) that the males during the breeding season are pale greenish yellow with dark spots and a pale vertebral streak, and are smaller than the females which are greyish-olive with dark spots.

This species, called by David *R. latrans*, because of its barking voice which is familiar during the monsoon, and generally known as the "bull frog," is very common throughout Southern India. The largest specimen in the Madras Museum measures 6 inches from the tip of the nose to the vent and 9 inches from the vent to the tip of the longest toe.

Specimens in the British and Madras Museums from Madras and the Nilgiris (7,000 feet).

In a note on the common Indian Otter, *Lutra nair*, Mr. Francis Day writes (*P.Z.S.*, 1873, p. 710): " Mr. Thomas had some otters of various sizes, which he had raised from babyhood in order to ascertain what their usual food is. When very young each consumed about one hundred frogs (*Rana cyanophlyctis*, Schn.) daily; but in April, when I saw them, they were about two-thirds grown; these small frogs were more difficult to procure, and they were having six to eight large bull frogs (*Rana tigrina*, Daud.) daily. This king amongst the frogs does not hesitate in eating those of the smaller species."

5. RANA GRACILIS.

Rana gracilis, *Wiegm. Nova. Acta. Ac. Leop.* 1835, p. 257; *Peters, Mon. Berl. Ac.* 1863, p. 78; *Günth. Rept. Brit. Ind.* 1864, p. 469, and *Proc. Zool. Soc.* 1875, p. 567; *Steindachn, Novara. Amph.* p. 18; *Stoliczka, Journ. As. Soc. Beng.* 1870, p. 142; *Anderson, Proc. Zool. Soc.* 1871, p. 200, and *Anat. Zool. Res. Yunnan*, 1878, p. 840; *Blgr. Cat.* 1882, p. 28.

Rana vittigera, *Günth. Cat.* 1858, p. 9.

? Rana nilagirica, *Jerdon, Journ. As. Soc. Beng.* 1853, p. 532.

Rana agricola, *Jerdon, l. c.*

Rana brevipalmata, *Peters, Mon. Berl. Ac.* 1871, p. 646.

Rana lymnocharis, (*Boie*) *Stoliczka, Proc. As. Soc. Beng.* 1872, p. 102, and *Journ. As. Soc. Beng.* 1873, p. 116.

" Very closely allied to *R. tigrina*, from which it differs chiefly in its smaller size, half webbed toes, and the presence of a small outer metatarsal tubercle, which is, however, sometimes indistinct. The relative length of the hind limb is very variable." (*Blgr*). As regards the colour and marking of this species, these are described by Günther (*Rept. Brit. Ind.*) as " greyish olive with large dark spots on the back and limbs ; a triangular transverse spot between the eyes, with the point directed backwards, is always present. A white vertebral line is rarely wanting. Five broad short bands radiate from the orbit, forming two spots below the eye ; the hinder band passes behind the tympanum. Uniform white below." This species is stated by Jerdon (*l.c. R. Nilagirica*) to have been seen by him only in marshes in the Wynaad and Nilgiris ; whereas his *R. agricola* is said (*l.c.*) to be found in inundated paddy fields and meadows and to be of a greenish colour mottled with darker.

The presence of the triangular transverse spot between the eyes noted by Günther is by no means constant.

Specimens in the British Museum from Madras, Malabar, and the Nilgiris; in the Madras Museum from the Nilgiris (5,000 feet). Measurements of one specimen :—length of body $2\frac{7}{10}$ inches, length of hind leg $3\frac{1}{4}$ inches.

6. RANA VERRUCOSA [PLATE IV, 2].

Rana verrucosa, *Günth. Proc. Zool. Soc.* 1875, p. 567 ; *Blgr. Cat.* 1882, p. 29, pl. IV, fig. 1.

Upper parts with numerous very prominent warts, tubercles and short glandular folds ; first finger extending much beyond the second ; toes nearly completely webbed, but the web does not extend to the extremity of the fourth toe. Colour and markings (of spirit specimens) : grey or brown above, darker spotted ; hinder side of thighs black, white marbled ; sometimes a broad light vertebral stripe.

Specimens in the British Museum from Malabar.

7. RANA RUFESCENS.

Rana rufescens, *Blgr. Cat.* 1882, p. 29.

Pyxicephalus rufescens, *Jerdon, Journ. As. Soc. Beng.* 1853, p. 534 ; *Günth. Rept. Brit. Ind.* 1864, p. 412.

Skin of the upper parts with large, rounded, very prominent warts ; inner metatarsal tubercle shovel-shaped ; toes webbed at the base. Colour and markings (of spirit specimens) : greyish brown above, indistinctly marbled ; legs transversely barred ; throat brown-spotted, with a M shaped blackish patch in the male. Described by Jerdon (*l.c.*) as being of rufous colour above, whitish beneath ; body rough and granulose ; limbs barred ; length $1\frac{1}{2}$ inches ; hind leg $2\frac{1}{10}$; foot $\frac{6}{10}$. Not rare in gardens on the Malabar Coast.

Specimens in the British Museum from Malabar.

8. RANA BREVICEPS [PLATE IV. 3].

Rana breviceps, *Schneid, Hist. Amph.* 1, p. 142 ; *Peters, Mon. Berl. Ac.* 1863, p. 76 ; *Blgr. Cat.* 1882, p. 32.

Sphærotheca strigata, *Günth. Cat.* 1858, p. 20, pl. II, fig. A.

Tomopterna delalandii, *Günth. l.c.*, p. 129.

Tomopterna strigata, *Günth. Proc. Zool. Soc.* 1860, p. 165.

Pyxicephalus fodiens, *Jerdon, Journ. As. Soc. Beng.* 1853, p. 534.

Pyxicephalus pluvialis, *Jerdon, l.c.*, p. 534.

Pyxicephalus breviceps, *Günth. Rept. Brit. Ind.* 1864, p. 411 ; *Theobald, Cat. Rept. As. Soc. Mus.*, p. 80 ; *Anderson, Proc. Zool. Soc.* 1871, p. 200.

Habit stout ; head short ; snout rounded ; tympanum half the size of the eye ; toes half-webbed ; inner metatarsal tubercle shovel-shaped, nearly as long as the second toe ; skin of the upper parts smooth, with some scattered tubercles. Colour and markings (of spirit specimens): light brown or olive above, darker marbled ; often a light vertebral stripe, and sometimes another on the upper side of each flank ; throat of the males blackish, that of the females generally brown-spotted.

4

Specimens in the British Museum from Madras and Malabar; in the Madras Museum from Tinnevelly.

The two species, *Pyxicephalus fodiens* and *P. pluvialis,* of Jerdon are not separated by Boulenger, who considers them as belonging to the same species. The former (*P. fodiens*) is described by Jerdon (*l.c.*) as being " greenish marbled with brown; length two inches; hind leg $2\frac{7}{10}$ths; foot $\frac{8}{10}$ths. Found in the Carnatic; burrows in the ground for $1\frac{1}{2}$ feet or so," while of the latter (*P. pluvialis*) Jerdon says that it is " nearly allied to the last; differs in its shorter thick form and shorter limbs; light greenish fawn, with dark marbling. Length of one, $2\frac{7}{10}$ths; hind leg, $2\frac{7}{10}$ths; feet $\frac{8}{10}$ths. I only procured this during the monsoon in the Carnatic. It is very different in appearance, though with so few essential distinctions, and the natives give a distinct name to each."

As regards this species Günther says (*Rept. Brit. Ind. P. breviceps*) : " The largest specimens measure 2 inches or somewhat more in length; their hind legs $2\frac{1}{4}$ or $2\frac{1}{2}$ inches, the males having the toes a little more slender than the females . . . . With the aid of its shovel likes metatarsal tubercle it burrows in the ground to a depth of $1\frac{1}{2}$ feet.

" We have seen coloured figures of Mr. Jerdon's *Pyxicephalus fodiens* and *P. pluvialis,* in the possession of Walter Elliot, Esq., from which it is evident that they are identical; the figure representing the *P. pluvialis* is taken from a male."

9. Rana dobsonii [Plate IV. 4].

Rana dobsonii, *Blgr. Cat.* 1882, p. 32, pl. III., fig. 1.

Habit stout; head large; tympanum two-thirds the size of the eye; toes webbed at the base; inner metatarsal tubercle shovel-shaped; skin smooth above, granulated on the belly. Colour and markings (of spirit specimen): grey above indistinctly marbled with brown; a deep black vitta along the canthus rostralis through the eye to the shoulder, expanding into a round spot on the tympanum; thighs black above, white marbled; beneath yellowish, indistinctly brown-spotted on the throat.

Specimens in the British Museum collected by Mr. G. E. Dobson at Mangalore, and by Colonel Beddome in South Canara.

10. Rana beddomii [Plate V. 1. A.B.].

Rana beddomii, *Blgr. Cat.* 1882, p. 55.

Polypedates beddomii, *Günth. Proc. Zool. Soc.* 1875, p. 571, pl. LXIII, fig. B.

Polypedates brachytarsus, *Günth. l.c.*, p. 572.

A free, pointed, conical papilla on the middle of the tongue; tympanum two-thirds the width of the eye; toes two-thirds webbed; tips of fingers and toes dilated into small discs; skin of the back with short longitudinal glandular folds; a strong glandular fold from the eye to the shoulder; lower surfaces smooth. Colour and markings (of spirit specimens): light brown above, indistinctly spotted; sometimes a light vertebral stripe; a dark cross band between the eyes; a black band along the canthus rostralis and a black temporal spot; limbs more or less distinctly cross-barred; beneath immaculate.

Specimens in the British Museum from Malabar, Travancore, Sivagiri, the Anamallays, and North Canara. A single specimen in the Madras Museum from Tinnevelly; length of body 2 inches, hind leg 4½ inches.

11. RANA SEMIPALMATA [PLATE V. 2].

Rana semipalmata, *Blgr. Cat.* 1882, p. 56, pl. IV, fig. 3.

This species is stated by Boulenger to be intermediate between *R. beddomii* and *R. leptodactyla*, differing from both by the much larger tympanum; from the former by the toes, which are only half-webbed; from the latter by the length of the first finger, which is superior to that of the second, and by the more extensive web between the toes.

Specimens in the British Museum from Malabar.

12. RANA LEPTODACTYLA.

Rana leptodactyla, *Blgr. Cat.* 1882, p. 57.
Polypedates brevipalmatus, *Günth. Proc. Zool. Soc.* 1875, p. 573.

Tongue with a free, pointed, conical papilla in the middle; tympanum half the width of the eye; toes one-third webbed; tips of fingers and toes dilated into small discs; skin of the back generally with short longitudinal glandular folds; lower surface smooth.

Specimens in the British Museum from Malabar and the Anamallays.

13. RANA DIPLOSTICTA [PLATE V. 3].

Rana diplosticta, *Blgr. Cat.* 1882, p. 58.
Ixalus diplostictus, *Günth. Proc. Zool. Soc.* 1875, p. 574, pl. LXIII, fig. C.

"Closely allied to, and perhaps not different from, the preceding. The canthus rostralis is perhaps more angular and the loreal regions not quite so oblique. A black spot above the loin." (*Blgr.*) "Tongue with a free, pointed papilla in the anterior part of the median line. Tympanum distinct, not quite half the size of the eye; skin of the back with some longitudinal folds. A cutaneous fold along the tarsus, commencing from the single metatarsal tubercle; fingers quite free; toes slender, with a very short web. Discs small; pinkish olive coloured, with a black line along the canthus rostralis, broader behind the eye, and continued over the tympanum. Symmetrical black spots on the sides—one in front of the axil, another on the middle of the sides of the trunk, a third above the loin; one or the other of these spots may be absent. Legs with dark cross-bars; anal region and soles of the feet black. Abdomen light coloured; throat sometimes mottled with brown." (*Günth. l.c. I. diplostictus.*)

Specimens in the British Museum from Malabar.

14. RANA PHRYNODERMA.

Rana phrynoderma, *Blgr. Cat.* 1882, p. 462.

Tongue with a free, pointed, conical papilla in the middle. Tympanum rather indistinct, about two-thirds the diameter of the eye. Fingers and toes rather short, the tips dilated into small discs; first finger not extending as far as second; toes one-fourth webbed; a small oval, inner metatarsal tubercle. Upper parts covered with warts of different sizes, and short glandular folds. Colour and markings (of spirit specimens): dark greyish brown above, with obsolete darker spots; limbs with regular cross-bars; beneath brown, dotted with whitish.

Specimens in the British Museum from the Anamallays.

15. RANA MALABARICA.

Rana malabarica, (Blgr.) Tschudi, Batr. p. 80; Dum. and Bibr. p. 635, pl. 86, fig. 1; Blgr. Cat. 1882, p. 60.

Hylarana malabarica, Günth. Rept. Brit. Ind. 1864, p. 426; Stoliczka, Proc. As. Soc. Beng. 1872, p. 105.

Tympanum very distinct, nearly as large as the eye; first finger extending beyond second; toes rather short, half-webbed; tips of fingers and toes swollen; inner metatarsal tubercle oval, blunt; a large rounded tubercle at the base of the fourth toe. Colour and markings (of spirit specimens): upper part of the head and back bright vinaceous red (brick-red during life), sometimes with a few black specks; sides of head and body and upper part of limbs blackish brown, the latter beautifully marbled with whitish; flanks with a series of white spots, sometimes confluent; a white line on the upper lip; beneath whitish, immaculate or brown-spotted, the spots sometimes covering nearly entirely the throat and breast.

Specimens in the British and Madras Museums from Malabar; length of body $2\frac{1}{8}$ inches, hind leg $3\frac{2}{3}$ inches.

16. RANA CURTIPES.

Rana curtipes, Jerdon, Journ. As. Soc. Beng. 1853, p. 532; Blgr. Cat. 1882, p. 61.

Pachybatrachus robustus, Mivart. Proc. Zool. Soc. 1868, p. 557.

Clinotarsus robustus, Mivart. Proc. Zool. Soc. 1869, p. 227.

Hylarana curtipes, Jerdon, Proc. As. Soc. 1870, p. 83.

Head large; tympanum distinct, as large as the eye; toes rather short, nearly entirely webbed; tips of fingers and toes swollen; a small, oval, inner metatarsal tubercle; a rather large, flat tubercle at the base of the fourth toe. Colour and markings (of spirit specimens): grey or brown above, with or without blackish dots; lateral fold margined with blackish; a blackish oblique spot below the eye; light brown beneath, the throat sometimes dark brown.

This species is said by Jerdon to be found in forest only, and chiefly seen during the monsoon, and to have a very peculiar, rather pleasing call. Its head and back are described by him as being bright buff above, sides deep maroon, legs dark purple with a few white spots, and abdomen white mottled. The observation has been made by Boulenger that the recently transformed young have on each side of the back, behind the tympanum, a very distinct parotoid gland, which generally disappears with age, though he has seen it quite distinct in a nearly adult female.

Specimens in the British Museum from North Canara and Malabar; in the Madras Museum from the Wynaad.

17. RANA TEMPORALIS [PLATE V. 4].

Rana temporalis, *Blgr. Cat.* 1882, p. 63.
Rana malabarica,[1] part *Günth. Cat.* 1858, p. 11.
Hylarana malabarica, *Kelaart, Prodr. Faun. Zeylan.* I. 1852, p. 191.
? Rana flavescens, *Jerdon, Journ. As. Soc. Beng.* 1853, p. 531.
Hylarana temporalis, *Günth. Rept. Brit. Ind.* 1864, p. 427, pl.
XXVI. fig. G, and *Proc. Zool. Soc.* 1875, p. 569.
Hylarana flavescens, *Jerdon, Proc. As. Soc. Beng.* 1870, p. 83.

Tympanum very distinct, three-fourths the size of the eye; toes nearly entirely webbed; tips of fingers and toes dilated into rather large discs; inner metatarsal tubercle small, oval; a small outer metatarsal tubercle. Colour and markings (of spirit specimens): brown above; loreal and temporal regions, and sometimes also the sides of the body, dark brown; limbs distinctly cross-barred; throat and breast more or less speckled with brown. The male has an oval flat gland on the inner side of the arm.

Specimens in the British Museum from Malabar and the Anamallays; in the Madras Museum from the Anamallays, and Nilgiris, the latter found on a tree-fern by the margin of a stream near Coonoor : length of body 3 inches, hind leg 5½ inches. In one of the specimens from the Nilgiris the throat and breast were scarcely, and in the other densely speckled with brown. The hinder side of the thighs was brown, with yellow marbling.

2. RHACOPHORUS.[2]

Synopsis of Species.

1. *Fingers not more than one-third webbed ; vomerine teeth between the choanæ.*

a. Tympanum distinct, more than half the width of the eye.

Belly granular; nostril much nearer the tip of the snout than the eye; tibio-tarsal articulation reaching the tip of the snout.
1. maculatus, p. 31.

b. Tympanum distinct, not more than half the width of the eye; nostril equally distant from the eye and the tip of the snout.

Fingers very distinctly webbed; hinder side of thighs brown, speckled with white.
2. pleurostictus, p. 30.

2. *Three outer fingers nearly entirely webbed ; toes nearly webbed.*
Discs of fingers and toes smaller than the tympanum.
3. lateralis, p. 32.

---

[1] A species, which is not recognised by Boulenger, was recorded by Jerdon (*Journ. As. Soc. Beng.* 1853, p. 531) as *Rana malabarica*, and described as being found only on the West Coast, and chiefly during the monsoon when it enters houses, and makes a great gobbling so much like a turkey that some people call it the 'Turkey frog.'

[2] Concerning this genus Boulenger says (Cat. 1882, p. 8) : " Had not the species been so numerous, I would have hesitated to separate *Rana* from *Rhacophorus*, which I characterise by the presence of a more or less developed web between the fingers. Though both genera pass into each other and constitute an uninterrupted series of species, I think that division convenient, it being easy to ascertain whether the fingers are quite free or webbed."

3. *Fingers entirely webbed.*

a. Vomerine teeth in two series on a level with the front edges of the choanæ.

Heel with a dermal appendage ; no spots.   4. *malabaricus*, p. 32.

b. Vomerine teeth in two oblique series between, and extending backwards a little beyond the choanæ.

Fingers and toes webbed to the discs, which are as large as the tympanum.   5. *beddomii*, p. 32.

1. Rhacophorus pleurostictus [Plate VI. 1].

Rhacophorus pleurostictus, *Blgr. Cat.* 1882, p. 79.
Polypedates pleurostictus, *Günth. Rept. Brit. Ind.* 1864, p. 430, pl. XXVI, fig. 1.
? Polypedates variabilis, *Jerdon, Journ. As. Soc. Beng.* 1853, p. 532.

Tympanum small, indistinct, not quite one-third the width of the eye ; fingers very distinctly webbed at the base ; discs well-developed ; toes broadly webbed, the interdigital membrane extending to the discs of the third and fifth toes ; metatarsus with a single tubercle. Colour and markings (of spirit specimens) : greenish or greyish above, with or without dark insuliform spots ; skin of the back smooth, of the sides and the belly finely granular ; flanks and hinder sides of thighs brown, the former marbled, the latter speckled with white.

For the following note on living specimens of this species I am indebted to Mr. J. R. Henderson :—

" Very variable in colour ; the following descriptions apply to very dark, and very light specimens respectively.

a. " Ground colour yellow, with many large bands and spots of a rich chocolate brown edged with black, and also a few orange spots. Smaller brownish spots are found between the large colour markings. Limbs banded transversely with chocolate brown. Under surface greyish with a few dark mottlings on the throat.

b. " Ground colour light brown, with the bands and spots of a slightly darker tint, and edged with black, sometimes minute creamy white spots on back. Under surface white with the mottlings on the throat almost obsolete or well marked. Limbs banded with brown transverse markings. The spots on the sides of the body considerably darker than on the back or bright yellow.

" The commonest species of 'Tree Frog' at Kotagiri ; frequently found in gardens, about water butts, &c. Young specimens are yellowish green, and have only a few dark markings."

There can be very little doubt that this species is the same as the *P. variabilis* of Jerdon, who calls it the green frog of the Nîlgiris, and describes it as a green frog, " sometimes unspotted, at other times with gold spots or blackish spots ; at times golden yellow with brown spots ; at other times brown with darker spots.

Length 2½ inches ; hind leg 4 ; foot 1$\frac{7}{10}$ths. Found in the Nîlgiris, in the banks of streams and in shrubs."

According to Günther *R. pleurostictus* (*l.c. Polypedates pleurostictus*) is very similar to *R. microtympanum* (*l.c. Polypedates microtympanum*), a species which is peculiar to Ceylon, but differs from it in having the fingers distinctly, instead of only slightly webbed.

Specimens in the British Museum from Madras, Ootacamund, Malabar, and the Anamallays; in the Madras Museum from the Nilgiris (6,000 feet): length of body 2½ inches, hind leg 3¾ inches.

2. RHACOPHORUS MACULATUS.

Rhacophorus maculatus, *Blgr. Cat.* 1882, p. 83.
Hyla maculata, *Gray, Ind. Zool.*
Hyla leucomystax, *Gravenh. Delic.* p 26.

Polypedates leucomystax, *Jerdon, Journ. As. Soc. Beng.* 1853, p. 532; *Tschudi, Batr.* p. 75; *Dum. and Bibr.* p. 519; *Kelaart, Prodr. Faun. Zeyl.* 1852, p. 193.

Bürgeria maculata, *Tschudi, l.c.*
Polypedates rugosus, *Dum. and Bibr.*, p. 520.
Polypedates cruciger, *Blyth. in Kelaart, Prodr. App.* p. 48.
Polypedates megacephalus, *Hallow, Proc. Ac. Philad.* 1860, p. 48.

Polypedates maculatus, *Günth. Rept. Brit. Ind.* 1864, p. 428; *Blanford, Journ. As. Soc. Beng.* 1870, p. 376; *Anderson, Proc. Zool. Soc.* 1871, p. 307; *Stoliczka, Proc. As. Soc. Beng.* 1872, p. 106.
Polypedates biscutiger, *Peters, Mon. Berl. Ac.* 1871, p. 649.

Tympanum nearly as large as the eye; toes nearly entirely, fingers slightly webbed; discs of fingers and toes well-developed, about half the diameter of the tympanum; a single, small, inner metatarsal tubercle. Skin smooth above, strongly granular on the belly and under the thighs; a narrow fold above the tympanum. Colour and markings (of spirit specimens): greyish or brown above, with or without brown spots and a large hour-glass-shaped figure on the hinder part of the head and the front part of the back; legs cross-barred; hinder side of thighs brown, with round white spots.

" The coloration " says Günther (*l.c. Polypedates maculatus*) " varies; the most constant markings are brownish cross-bars on the limbs, small, more or less distinct, round white or whitish spots on the hinder side of the thigh, and a more or less developed white streak on the upper lip. This species has the power of changing its colours; it is sometimes buff above, sometimes ashy-grey, chocolate-brown, tinged with rose or lilac, black spots being more or less visible."

The hind limbs of a specimen in the Madras Museum are perfectly white, without markings.

This is the familiar frog which is so frequently seen in Madras at night, adhering to vertical surfaces, *e.g.*, walls and windows, by means of the discs on its fingers and toes, and commonly known among Europeans as the chunam frog, from the frequency with which it is found on chunam (shell-lime) walls.

Specimens in the British Museum from the lower slopes of the Nilgiris, Malabar, Salem, and Madras; in the Madras Museum from Madras, and the Shevaroys (5,000 feet).

3. RHACOPHORUS MALABARICUS.

Rhacophorus malabaricus, *Jerdon, Proc. As. Soc. Beng.* 1870, p. 84 ; *Blgr. Cat.* 1882, p. 90. *Woodcut.*
Hyla reinwardtii, part. *Schleg. Abbild.* p. 105, pl. 30, fig. 3.
Rhacophorus reinwardtii, part. *Dum. & Bibr.* p. 532, pl. 89, fig. 1.

Fingers entirely webbed ; heel with a dermal appendage ; granules under the thighs intermixed with larger ones. Colour and markings (of spirit specimens) : purplish above, often speckled all over with blackish ; no spots on the sides of the body, or on the membrane between the fingers and toes.

This species, according to Boulenger, is very closely allied to, and differs chiefly by coloration from *R. reinwardtii*, concerning which species Jerdon says (*l.c.*, p. 84) "I recorded *Rhacophorus reinwardtii* apud. *Dum. and Bibr.*, from Malabar in my catalogue [1], whence it was also procured by the French collectors. . . . . Major Beddome has sent me a specimen, on comparing which with Khasi specimens a perceptible difference is apparent. The head and body of the Malabar are indistinctly, though finely, tuberculated ; the habit is more slender, and there is a distinct fold of skin over the eye in *reinwardtii*, absent in this. The head too is perhaps a trifle longer. I shall provisionally call it *Rhacophorus malabaricus*. It has the spots on the sides of the body so conspicuous in Khasi specimens of *reinwardtii*.

Specimens in the British Museum from Malabar.

4. RHACOPHORUS BEDDOMII.

Rhacophorus beddomii, *Blgr. Cat.* 1882, p. 468.

Tympanum two-fifths the width of the eye ; fingers and toes webbed to the discs, which are as large as the tympanum ; a small inner metatarsal tubercle ; upper surface with very small smooth tubercles ; beneath granulate. Colour and markings (of spirit specimens) : light reddish brown above, indistinctly variegated with grey. From snout to vent 49 mm.

A specimen in the British Museum from the Calcad hills, Tinnevelly (3,000 feet).

5. RHACOPHORUS LATERALIS.

Rhacophorus lateralis, *Blgr. Ann. Mag. Nat. Hist.* Ser. 5, Vol. XII. 1883, p. 162.

Tympanum half the diameter of the eye ; three outer fingers nearly entirely webbed ; toes nearly entirely webbed ; discs of fingers and toes smaller than the tympanum ; a rather indistinct inner metatarsal tubercle ; skin smooth, granular on the belly and under the thighs. Colour and markings (of spirit specimens): purplish above, white beneath ; head and back with dark dots ; coloured parts of limbs with dark cross lines ; a white streak on each side from the nostril along the outer edge

---

[1] "Rhachophorus Reinwardtii, *Dum. and Bibr.* Found in the Malabar Coast on trees, and in grass during the monsoon. Not very common." *Jerdon, Journ. As. Soc. Beng.* 1853, p. 532.

of the upper eyelid to the groin; arm, the three inner fingers, and the four inner toes not coloured.

A single young specimen recorded from Malabar.

3. IXALUS.

Synopsis of Species.

1. *Fingers free or very slightly webbed.*

A. *Tongue with a free, pointed papilla in the anterior part of the median line.*

1. Toes more than half-webbed.

A glandular lateral fold; toes nearly entirely webbed, with small discs.   1. *opisthorhodus*, p. 34.

No glandular lateral fold; toes very broadly webbed, with large discs.   2. *saxicola*, p. 35.

2. Toes not more than half-webbed.

Tibio-tarsal articulation not reaching beyond the eye; toes webbed at the base.   3. *glandulosus*, p. 37.

Tibio-tarsal articulation reaching beyond the eye; toes half-webbed.   4. *chalazodes*, p. 38.

Tibio-tarsal articulation not reaching the eye; toes half-webbed.   5. *flavicentris*, p. 38.

Snout sub-acuminate.   6. *signatus*, p. 38.

B. *Tongue without papilla.*

1. Skin smooth above and beneath; a glandular lateral fold; tympanum indistinct.

Toes entirely webbed.   7. *fuscus*, p. 34.

Toes one-third or two-fifths webbed.   8. *silvaticus*, p. 35.

2. Skin smooth above, or with small tubercles; no glandular lateral fold.

a. Tympanum distinct.

α. Tympanum at least half the width of the eye.

Tympanum half the width of the eye; toes half-webbed; discs moderate.   9. *leucorhinus*, p. 35.

β. Tympanum not half the width of the eye.

Tympanum about one-third the size of the eye; toes less than one-third webbed; tibio-tarsal articulation reaching beyond the eye.   10. *punctatus*, p. 37.

b. Tympanum indistinct or quite hidden.

a. Snout slightly pointed.

Toes half webbed.   11. *pulcher*, p. 36.

β. Snout rounded.

Tibio-tarsal articulation reaching beyond the eye; toes two-thirds webbed; hinder side of thighs not coloured.   12. *femoralis*, p. 35.

Tibio-tarsal articulation not extending beyond the eye; toes half-webbed; hinder side of thighs not coloured.   13. *beddomii*, p. 36.

5

Tibio tarsal articulation reaching beyond the eye; toes two-thirds webbed; hinder side of thighs coloured. 14. *variabilis*, p. 36.

1. IXALUS OPISTHORHODUS [PLATE VI. 2. A.B.].

Ixalus opisthorhodus, *Günth. Proc. Zool. Soc.* 1868, p. 484, pl. XXXVII, fig. 3; *Blgr. Cat.* 1882, p. 95.

? Limnodytes ? phyllophila, *Jerdon, Journ. As. Soc. Beng.* 1853, p. 532, and *Proc. As. Soc. Beng.* 1870, p. 85.

Tongue with a free pointed papilla in the median line; fingers free; toes nearly entirely webbed; discs small; a small inner metatarsal tubercle. Colour and markings (of spirit specimens) : brownish above, with a few indistinct darker markings; loreal and temporal regions dark brown; limbs cross-barred; lower surface of hind limbs, hinder sides of thighs, and sometimes hind part of belly beautifully rose-coloured.

For the following note on living specimens of this species, I am indebted to Mr. J. R. Henderson : " Colour of upper surface dark-brown, lighter on the sides; under surface yellowish with a series of dark mottlings, which almost entirely cover the throat, and render it dark. Lower surface of the hind limbs rose-coloured; anal region black. A very conspicuous black band on each side of the head under each eye and nostril, and continued in some specimens into the forelimb. A few whitish tubercles occasionally present on the sides. Two longitudinal folds always present on the trunk, and a few indistinct wrinkles on the head, back, and hind legs.

Common in densely wooded sholas near Kotagiri (6,000 feet), and at Rungaswamy's pillar. Lives in the margins of shaded streams, and takes freely to the water."

It is possible that this species is the same as Jerdon's *Limnodytes phyllophila*,—n.s., which is described (*Journ. As. Soc. Beng.* 1853, p. 532) as a small frog with the sub-digital discs very slightly dilated; toes not quite completely webbed; tympanum small; reddish yellow, with the sides of the face dark purple; found in all the western forests among decayed leaves.

Specimens in the British Museum from the Nilgiris and Malabar; in the Madras Museum from Kotagiri (6,000 feet) : length of body $1\frac{1}{16}$ inch, hind leg $1\frac{2}{3}$ inch.

2. IXALUS FUSCUS [PLATE VI. 5].

Ixalus fuscus, *Blgr. Cat.* 1882, pl. 96, pl. X, fig. 3.

Tongue without a papilla; tympanum small, indistinct; fingers free; toes entirely webbed; discs small; a small inner metatarsal tubercle; skin smooth above and beneath; a narrow glandular lateral fold. Colour and markings (of spirit specimens) : brown above; sides of head and body generally darker; limbs cross-barred; hinder side of thighs dark-brown, with a more or less accentuated light stripe along the middle; whitish beneath, marbled with brown. From snout to vent 32 mm.

Specimens in the British Museum from Travancore, Torocata, the Anamallays, Sivagiri, Malabar, and North Canara.

3. IXALUS SILVATICUS.

Ixalus silvaticus, *Blgr. Cat.* 1882, p. 469.

Tongue without a papilla; tympanum small, indistinct; fingers free, toes one-third or two-fifths webbed, the membrane extending as a narrow fringe along their sides; a small inner metatarsal tubercle; skin smooth above and beneath; a narrow glandular lateral fold. Colour and markings (of spirit specimens): brown above, with rather indistinct darker markings, the most constant being a broad chevron between the eyes; sides of head blackish brown; limbs cross-barred; hinder side of thighs blackish brown, groin and front of thighs frequently rose-coloured; brown beneath, throat and chest dotted, belly and lower surface of hind limbs marbled with whitish. From snout to vent 27 mm.

Specimens in the British Museum from Malabar.

4. IXALUS SAXICOLA.

Ixalus saxicola, *Blgr. Cat.* 1882, p. 97.
Polypedates ? saxicola, *Jerdon, Journ. As. Soc. Beng.* 1853, p. 533.

Tongue with a free, pointed papilla in the middle line; tympanum small, hidden; fingers free, toes very broadly webbed; discs large; a small inner metatarsal tubercle. Colour and markings (of spirit specimens): olive brown above, with more or less distinct darker reticulations; limbs cross-barred; throat and breast often marbled with brown.

This species is described by Jerdon (*l.c. Polypedates ? saxicola*) as being found on rocks in shady mountain streams in Malabar and the Wynaad; dark olive green with dark marbling, and barred limbs.

Specimens in the British and Madras Museums from Malabar.

5. IXALUS LEUCORHINUS [PLATE VI. 3].

Ixalus leucorhinus, *Günth. Cat.* 1858, p. 75; *Martens. Nomencl. Rept. Mus. Berol.* 1856, p. 36; *Blgr. Cat.* 1882, p. 98.
Ixalus temporalis, *Günth. Rept. Brit. Ind.* 1864, p. 434, pl. XXVI, fig. E.

Tongue without a papilla; tympanum distinct, half the width of the eye; fingers very slightly, toes half webbed; discs moderate; a small inner metatarsal tubercle. Skin smooth above, granular beneath. Colour and markings (of spirit specimens): yellowish brown or olive above; a dark stripe below the canthus rostralis and on the temporal region; sometimes a large hexagonal light spot on the snout; generally a dark vitta between the eyes, and another arched one on each side of the back; sometimes a light vertebral line or stripe, extending or not along the hind limbs; throat generally dotted with brown, sometimes quite brown with an immaculate median line.

Specimens in the British Museum from Malabar and North Canara.

6. IXALUS FEMORALIS [PLATE VI. 4].

Ixalus femoralis, *Günth. Rept. Brit. Ind.* 1864, p. 434, pl. XXVI, fig. D; *Blgr. Cat.* 1882, p. 101.
Ixalus pulchellus, *Günth. Ann. Mag. Nat. Hist.* 1872, ser. 4, Vol. IX, p. 88.
Ixalus fergusoni, *Günth. eod. loc.* 1876, Vol. XVII, p. 379.

Tongue without a papilla ; snout rounded ; tympanum small, hidden ; fingers slightly, toes two-thirds webbed ; discs moderate ; a very small inner metatarsal tubercle ; skin smooth or minutely granular above ; beneath granular, the granules very large on the belly. Colour and markings (of spirit specimens) : above bluish green, purple or brownish, immaculate or with black specks ; arms colourless, thighs with a stripe of pigment on its upper surface. Single specimens are recorded by Boulenger, in one of which the upper surface had a few large reddish brown spots, while in another the hinder side of the thighs were black-spotted.

Recorded in the British Museum Catalogue from Ceylon. Several specimens in the Madras Museum, without any record of the locality in which they were found. The upper surfaces of the body and lower leg of one specimen uniformly violet coloured.

7. IXALUS BEDDOMII [PLATE VII. 1].

Ixalus beddomii, *Gunth. Proc. Zool. Soc.* 1875, p. 575 ; *Blgr. Cat.* 1882, p. 101, pl. X, fig. 7.

Tongue without a papilla ; tympanum small, hidden ; snout rounded ; fingers free, toes half-webbed ; discs moderate ; a small inner metatarsal tubercle. Skin smooth above, granular beneath. Colour and markings (of spirit specimens) : uniform greenish above ; thighs colourless, except a greenish stripe along their upper surface.

Specimens in the British Museum from Malabar, and Atray Mallay, Travancore (4,000 feet).

8. IXALUS PULCHER.

Ixalus pulcher, *Blgr. Cat.* 1882, p. 469.

Tongue without a papilla ; snout slightly pointed ; tympanum small and indistinct ; fingers with a rudiment of web ; toes half-webbed ; discs moderate ; a very small inner metatarsal tubercle. Skin smooth above, granular beneath. Colour and markings (of spirit specimens) : blue-green or purplish above, generally uniform, sometimes with small black spots ; a purplish brown streak on canthus rostralis and generally on post-ocular fold ; loreal region white, uniform or with purplish brown spots, or purplish brown, dotted or not with whitish ; arms, and generally forearms, colourless ; thighs with a stripe of pigment on their upper surface. From snout to vent 23 mm.

Specimens in the British Museum from Manantoddy.

9. IXALUS VARIABILIS [PLATE VII. 2].

Ixalus variabilis, *Gunth. Cat.* 1858. p. 74, pl. IV, figs. A and B, and *Rept. Brit. Ind.* 1864, p. 433, and *Proc. Zool. Soc.* 1875, p. 573 ; *Blgr. Cat.* 1882, p. 102.

? Phyllomedusa ? wynaadensis, *Jerdon, Journ. As. Soc. Beng.* 1853, p. 533.

Tongue without a papilla ; snout rounded ; tympanum indistinct, about half the width of the eye ; fingers very slightly, toes two-thirds webbed ; discs moderate ; a small inner metatarsal tubercle. Skin smooth above, granular beneath. Colour and markings subject to great variations, the upper surface being bluish, greenish, brownish, or blackish, uniform, or variously spotted or speckled with darker or lighter.

A specimen in the Madras Museum captured at Ootacamund, was, during life, of a grass-green colour, plump, and had its legs tucked under it, forming an oval about 1 inch × ¾ inch.

This species, the "tinkling frog" of the Nilgiris, is described by Jerdon (*l.c.*) as being found in grass and among bushes on the Nilgiris, and having a peculiar loud clear metallic tinkling call, and named by him *Phyllomedusa ? tinniens*, in which the tibio-tarsal joint only reaches the end of the tympanum, when the hind leg is drawn forwards; whereas in *Ixalus variabilis* the tibio-tarsal joint reaches either between the eye and the tip of the snout, or even as far as the tip of the snout, and, in this respect, it corresponds to Jerdon's *Phyllomedusa ? wynaodensis.*

Very abundant at Ootacamund, and frequently heard during the monsoon, though seldom seen, and very difficult to capture. A friend writes to me : "We have over and over again offered a rupee a head for the tinkling frog, and never got one. The natives say that it is a regular ventriloquist, and that, when its tinkle seems to indicate that it is on your right hand, it is really on your left. This I fancy constitutes the difficulty of capture, as you can never be sure of its exact locality, and the moment you begin hunting for it, it stops tinkling, and hides."

Specimens in the British Museum from Malabar, Sivagiri, and Pycara ; in the Madras Museum from Ootacamund, (length of body 1 inch, hind legs 1½ inches) and Kotagiri (6,000 feet), the former found inside the flower of an Arum.

10. IXALUS GLANDULOSUS [PLATE VII. 3].

Ixalus glandulosus, *Jerdon, Journ. As. Soc. Beng.* 1853, p. 532 ; *Günth. Proc. Zool. Soc.* 1875, p. 573 ; *Blgr. Cat.* 1882, p. 103.

Ixalus montanus, *Günth. Proc. Zool. Soc.* 1875, p. 574, pl. LXVI, fig. A.

Tongue with a free, pointed papilla on the anterior part of the middle line ; tympanum small, hidden ; fingers free, toes webbed at the base ; discs moderate ; a small inner metatarsal tubercle. Skin of upper surfaces smooth or with small indistinct tubercles ; sides generally glandular ; lower surfaces granular. Colour and markings (of spirit specimens): dark purplish brown above, uniform, or with indistinct markings, or greyish brown, with symmetrical dark brown markings ; beneath immaculate or more or less spotted.

This species is described by Jerdon (*l.c.*) as "a small tree frog, with very obtuse muzzle, feet slightly webbed ; abdomen largely glandular, tympanum indistinct ; green above, yellowish on the sides and limbs ; length 1$\frac{7}{10}$ths ; hind leg $\frac{7}{10}$ths ; foot 3$\frac{2}{10}$ths."

Specimens in the British Museum from Travancore, Malabar, the Nilgiris, Anamallays, and Kudra Mukl (6,000 feet) ; in the Madras Museum from Kotagiri (6,000 feet).

11. IXALUS PUNCTATUS.

Ixalus punctatus, *Anderson, Journ. As. Soc.* 1871, p. 27 ; *Blgr. Cat.* 1882, p. 104.

Tongue without a papilla; snout rounded; tympanum distinct, about one-third the size of the eye; fingers free; toes less than one-third webbed; discs of fingers well developed, of toes smaller; a small inner metatarsal tubercle. Back nearly smooth, with a few scattered minute tubercles on the sacral region; finely tubercular on the sides and under surface of the body and thighs. Colour and markings (of spirit specimens): brownish above as far forwards as the anterior angle of the eye, where the brown abruptly ceases in a straight line, the upper surface of the snout being light olive; upper lip white; a dark brown band from the snout to the tympanum; sides bluish grey, the minute tubercles dark brown; under surfaces dirty yellowish, the chin, throat, and thorax with scattered brown spots.

Recorded in the British Museum Catalogue (1882) from the Nilgiris.

The type specimen in the Indian Museum, Calcutta, was described by Anderson (*l.c.*) from a specimen labelled " I. tinniens, *Jerdon* " from the Nilgiris.

12. IXALUS CHALAZODES [PLATE VII. 4].

Ixalus chalazodes, *Günth. Proc. Zool. Soc.* 1875, p. 574, pl. LXVI, fig. B; *Blgr. Cat.* 1882, p. 105.

Tongue with a free, pointed papilla in the median line; snout rounded; tympanum small, hidden; fingers free; toes half-webbed; discs moderate; a small inner metatarsal tubercle. The hind limb being carried forwards, the tibio-tarsal articulation reaches between the eye and the tip of the snout. Skin of upper parts smooth; a few round tubercles on the flanks, on the hind part of the back, and on the metatarsus; beneath granular. Colour and markings (of spirit specimen): uniform bluish green above, the round tubercles white.

A single specimen in the British Museum from Travancore; length of body 26 mm., hind limb 42 mm.

13. IXALUS FLAVIVENTRIS [PLATE VII. 5].

Ixalus flaviventris, *Blgr. Cat.* 1882, p. 105, pl. XI, fig. 1.

Tongue with a free, pointed papilla in the median line; snout rounded; fingers free; toes half-webbed; discs moderate; a very small inner metatarsal tubercle. The hind limb being carried forwards, the tibio-tarsal articulation reaches the eye. Skin smooth above, granular beneath. Colour and markings (of spirit specimens): above dark brown with round yellow spots, or brown with dark reticulations or spots; hinder side of thighs dark brown, with round yellow spots; lower surfaces yellow, marbled with brown.

Specimens in the British Museum from Malabar.

14. IXALUS SIGNATUS [PLATE VII. 6].

Ixalus signatus, *Blgr. Cat.* 1882, p. 106, pl. XI, fig. 2.

Tongue with a small papilla in the median line; snout sub-acuminate; tympanum small, hidden; fingers free; toes half-webbed; discs well developed. Skin smooth above, granular beneath. Colour and markings (of spirit specimens): greyish or brownish above; a dark cross band between the eyes, and a large X-shaped marking on the back; upper lip with a few white spots; limbs cross-barred; hinder side of thighs not coloured; sometimes with brown vermiculations; beneath immaculate.

Specimens in the British Museum from Malabar.

Specimens in the Madras Museum from Pycara and Coonoor (Nilgiris): length of body 1½ inch, hind leg 1⅞ inch; generally greenish yellow on upper surface with black or yellow markings; cross-bars on hind limbs brown. In a single specimen the colour of the upper surface was burnt red, fading to yellow on the thighs and sides.

4. NYCTIBATRACHUS.

"This new genus is related to *Rana* by the general characters, to *Rhacophorus* by the structure of the distal phalanges, but differs from both by the erect pupil." (*Blgr. Cat.*).

1. NYCTIBATRACHUS PYGMÆUS [PLATE VIII. 1].

Nyctibatrachus pygmæus, *Blgr. Cat.* 1882, p. 113, pl. XII, fig. 1.
Rana pygmæa, *Günth. Proc. Zool. Soc.* 1875, p. 568.

Habit stout; vomerine teeth in two small oblique series behind the level of the choanæ. Toes half-webbed, the tips swollen into very small discs; a small, blunt, oval, inner metatarsal tubercle. Skin smooth, with some glandular folds on the head and front part of the back. Colour and markings (of spirit specimens): dark brown above, with rather indistinct blackish markings; light brown beneath.

Specimens in the British Museum from the Anamallays. Also collected by Colonel Beddome in Malabar.

2. NYCTIBATRACHUS MAJOR [PLATE VIII. 2].

Nyctibatrachus major, *Blgr. Cat.* 1882, p. 114, pl. XII, fig. 2.

Habit stout; vomerine teeth in two straight series (oblique in the young), much behind the level of the choanæ. Toes nearly entirely webbed; tips of fingers and toes swollen into small discs; a small, elongate, scarcely prominent inner metatarsal tubercle. Above with very small, closely set vermiculated folds; upper eyelid covered with strong tubercles. Colour and markings (of spirit specimens): brown above, with rather indistinct darker and lighter markings; brownish beneath, more or less speckled with brown.

Specimens in the British Museum from Malabar and the Wynaad.

5. NANNOBATRACHUS.

1. NANNOBATRACHUS BEDDOMII.

1. Nannobatrachus beddomii, *Blgr. Cat.* 1882, p. 470.

Habit stout; pupil erect; vomerine teeth in two oblique oval groups behind the level of the choanæ; toes with a slight rudiment of a web; discs very small; a very indistinct inner metatarsal tubercle, skin quite smooth. Colour and markings (of spirit specimens): brown above, variegated with darker; generally a more or less defined light band on each side of the back; limbs cross-barred; whitish beneath, immaculate. From snout to vent 20 mm.

Specimens in the British Museum from Malabar and Tinnevelly.

2. ENGYSTOMATIDÆ.

Synopsis of the Genera.

I. *Precoracoids present.*

Coracoids moderate, horizontal. Pupil erect; tongue elliptical; palate without ridges.   1. Melanobatrachus, p. 40.

II. *No precoracoids.*

Pupil erect; tongue elliptical; tympanum hidden; toes more or less webbed.   2. Microhyla, p. 40.

Pupil erect; tongue oblong; palatine bones forming an acute ridge; tympanum hidden.   3. Callula, p. 41.

Pupil erect; tongue oval; two small bony prominences between the choanæ; toes webbed at the base.   4. Cacopus, p. 43.

1. MELANOBATRACHUS.

1. MELANOBATRACHUS INDICUS.

Melanobatrachus indicus, *Bedd. Proc. Zool. Soc.* 1878, p. 722; *Blgr. Cat.* 1882, p. 157.

Pupil erect; tongue elliptical; no tympanic disc; fingers short, first much shorter than second; toes rather short, one-third webbed; metatarsal tubercles very indistinct. Upper surface tubercular; sides and lower surface smooth. Colour and markings (of spirit specimens): black; tubercles of back greyish; belly dotted with greyish; a large whitish (scarlet) spot on the lower surface of the thigh.

The habitat of this species is described by Colonel Beddome (*l.c.*) as:—"The Anamallays and the Ghat range to the south of these mountains; very rare, in moist evergreen forests of 4,000 feet elevation, under old rotten logs. The specimens found were all in quite a torpid state, and curled up almost into a ball, but became very active when put in spirits." It is also regarded by Colonel Beddome from the Nilgiris in the *Manual of the Nilagiri District* (1880), where he says: "This little frog only lately discovered on the Ánémalés and Madura hills, has just been found at Walaghát."

Specimens in the British Museum from the Anamallays, 4,000 feet, and North Travancore; in the Madras Museum from the Anamallays: length of body 1½ inch, hind leg 1 1/16 inch.

2. MICROHYLA.

1. MICROHYLA RUBRA.

Microhyla rubra, *Blgr. Cat.* 1882, p. 164.
Diplopelma ornatum, part. *Günth. Cat.* 1858, p. 50.
Engystoma rubrum, *Jerdon, Journ. As. Soc. Beng.* 1853, p. 534.

Habit stout; pupil erect; tongue elliptical; tympanum hidden; toes one-third webbed; tips of fingers and toes not swollen; two rather large, oval, compressed, very prominent metatarsal tubercles. Skin smooth. Colour and markings (of spirit specimens): reddish brown above, sides darker; a dark brown line from the tip of the snout through the eye along the side of the back to the groin; a dark brown mark across the thigh, beginning on the loin; limbs with more or less distinct cross bars; sometimes a dark X-shaped marking on the front of the back, commencing between the eyes; beneath immaculate, or with a few brown dots on the throat.

This species is said by Jerdon (*l.c.*) to be found in the Carnatic near rivers and sandy banks, and is very common in Madras during the monsoon.

Specimens in the British Museum from Madras and South India : in the Madras Museum from the Nilgiris (6,000 feet), Tinnevelly and Madras : length of body 1 inch, hind leg 1⅔ inch.

2. MICROHYLA ORNATA.

Microhyla ornata, *Blgr. Cat.* 1882, p. 165.
Diplopelma ornatum, part. *Günth. Cat.* 1858, p. 50, and *Rept. Brit. Ind.* 1864, p. 417.
Engystoma ornatum, *Dum. & Bibr.*, p. 745.
Engystoma carnaticum, *Jerdon, Journ. As. Soc. Beng.* 1853, p. 534.
? Engystoma malabaricum, *Jerdon, l.c.*
Diplopelma carnaticum, *Stoliczka, Journ. As. Soc. Beng.* 1870, p. 154, pl. IX, fig. 5.

Habit moderately slender; pupil erect; tongue elliptical; tympanum hidden; toes rather slender, with a slight rudiment of web; tips of fingers and toes swollen into very small discs; two small metatarsal tubercles. Skin smooth. Colour and markings (of spirit specimens): reddish or greyish olive above, with a large dark marking on the back, beginning between the eyes, and becoming broader as it extends to the hind part of the body; on each side of this marking are undulating longitudinal dusky lines, which may be absent; a dark band along the side of the head and body; limbs with dark cross-bars; throat and chest generally greyish or brownish dotted with white; the remainder of the lower surfaces immaculate.

This species is said by Jerdon (*l.c.*) to be found in the Carnatic during the monsoon and has been recorded by Colonel Beddome (*Manual of the Nilagiri District*, 1880) from the Nilgiris (Walaghát).

Specimens in the British Museum from Madras : in the Madras Museum from Tinnevelly : length of body ⅘ inch, hind leg 1½ inch.

3. CALLULA.

Synopsis of Species.

I. *Toes at least one-third webbed.*

Tips of fingers dilated into well-developed discs; outer metatarsal tubercle minute.
1. *obscura*, p. 42.

6

II. *Toes webbed at the base.*

Metatarsal tubercles small, scarcely prominent. 2. *olivacea*, p. 42.

III. *Toes perfectly free.* 3. *triangularis*, p. 42.

1. CALLULA OBSCURA [PLATE VIII. 3].

Callula obscura, *Günth. Rept. Brit. Ind.* 1864, p. 438; *Blgr. Cat.* 1882, p. 169, pl. XIII, fig. 3.

Tips of fingers dilated into well-developed truncated discs; toes one-third or half-webbed, tips slightly swollen; two small metatarsal tubercles, the inner oval, blunt, scarcely prominent, the outer minute, rounded. Skin smooth, or with small flat tubercles on the head and back. Colour and markings (of spirit specimens): above brownish or greyish with blackish angular markings, sometimes uniform blackish-brown; beneath blackish-brown, spotted with whitish.

Specimens in the British Museum from Travancore, Malabar, and the Anamallays.

2. CALLULA OLIVACEA [PLATE VIII. 4].

Callula olivacea, *Günth. Proc. Zool. Soc.* 1875, p. 567, pl. LXIV, fig. B.

Fingers rather slender, the tips dilated, truncate; toes not dilated at the ends, with a slight rudiment of web; two small, scarcely prominent metatarsal tubercles, the inner elongate. Skin nearly smooth. Colour and markings (of spirit specimens): olive above, marbled with dark brown; belly whitish, immaculate.

Specimens in the British Museum from the Yellagherri hills, and the Godávari valley: in the Madras Museum from Madras, where this species has been found by Mr. J. R. Henderson, living in white-ant nests in his compound which adjoins that of the Museum. I have seen a single specimen in my own garden in Madras feeding on white-ants underneath a flower-pot.

3. CALLULA TRIANGULARIS [PLATE VIII. 5].

Callula triangularis, *Günth. Proc. Zool. Soc.* 1875, p. 576; *Blgr. Cat.* 1882, p. 171, pl. XIII, fig. 4.

Tips of fingers dilated into rather small truncated discs; toes perfectly free, the tips not dilated; two small metatarsal tubercles, inner one largest, oval, blunt. Skin smooth, or with some flat tubercles on the back. Colour and markings (of spirit specimens): light olive above, with a large triangular blackish spot occupying nearly the whole length of the backs; sides and lower surfaces blackish brown, latter spotted with whitish; limbs blackish brown with large light olive spots.

Specimens in the British Museum from Malabar and the Nilgiris; in the Madras Museum from Ootacamund (7,000 feet): length of body 31 mm., hind leg 40 mm.

4. CACOPUS.

1. CACOPUS SYSTOMA [PLATE IX. 1].

Cacopus systoma, *Günth. Rept. Brit. Ind.* 1864, p. 415 ; *Blgr. Cat.* 1882, p. 174 ; *Thurston, Proc. Zool. Soc.* 1st March 1887.
Uperodon marmoratum, *Günth. Cat.* 1858, p. 49 ; *Dum. & Bibr.* p. 749.
Rana systoma, *Schneid. Hist. Amph.* 1, p. 144 ; *Peters, Mon. Berl. Ac.* 1863, p. 82.
Engystoma marmoratum, *Cuv. R. A. ; Guerin. Icon. Rept.* pl. XXVII, fig. 3.
Systoma leschenhaultii, *Tschudi. Batr.* p. 86.
Systoma marmoratum, *Steindachn, Novara. Amph.* p. 36.
? Pachybatrachus Petersii, *Keferst. Arch. f. Naturg.* 1868, p. 274, pl. 6, figs. 8–10.

Habit stout ; snout rounded, without canthus rostralis ; inter-orbital space twice or not quite twice the width of the upper eyelid ; toes webbed at the base ; two strong, shovel-shaped metatarsal tubercles, the inner as long as the second toe. Skin smooth, upper surface sometimes tubercular. Colour and markings (of spirit specimens) : olive or pinkish brown above, marbled with blackish brown ; beneath whitish, immaculate.

This species, which has been recorded by Colonel Beddome (*Manual of the Nilagiri District*, 1880) from the slopes of the Nilgiris, can be found in large numbers at night in Madras compounds during the monsoon, emitting a characteristic sound. The male has an enormous sub-gular vocal sac. I have seen it in the month of January, apparently in a torpid state, buried in a hole, which it had excavated for itself, underneath flower-pots in my garden.

Specimens in the British Museum from Madras and the Balarangam hills ; in the Madras Museum from Madras and the Nilgiris. Colour of the upper surface of living specimens black or blackish brown with delicate primrose undulating marbling. Length of body $2\frac{7}{12}$ inches, hind leg $2\frac{1}{2}$ inches.

2. CACOPUS GLOBULOSUS [PLATE X. 1].

Cacopus globulosus, *Günth. Rept. Brit. Ind.* 1864, p. 416, pl. XXVI, fig. K ; *Anderson, Proc. Zool. Soc.* 1871, p. 201 ; *Blgr. Cat.* 1882, p. 175 ; *Thurston, Proc. Zool. Soc.* 1st March 1887.
Systoma globulosum, *Cope. Journ. Ac. Philad.* (2) VI. 1867, p. 194.

Globular ; habit stouter than the preceding ; snout longer with distinct canthus rostralis ; inter-orbital space three times the width of the upper eyelid ; inner metatarsal tubercle longer than the second toe. Colour and markings (of spirit specimens): brown, uniform, or spotted with darker.

Specimens in the British and Madras Museums from Russellkonda. The specimen in the Madras Museum (length of body $2\frac{3}{4}$ inches, hind leg $2\frac{7}{12}$ inches) has its stomach enormously distended by a mass of winged white-ants (*termites.*)

Günther says (*l.c.*) with respect to two specimens of this species from Russellkonda : " The younger is 13 lines long, the larger (a very old female) 34 lines long. The former is distended by fluid in an extraordinary manner, so that the body has the shape of a ball, from which the head and limbs project. The fluid is contained in the abdominal cavity. The larger individual is distended in a similar way, but this is caused by an extraordinary development of the ovaria; these organs become so large, that, not having room in the abdominal cavity, *they extend right across the back, where they coalesce*, so that the body of the animal is entirely surrounded by the mass of the ovaries."

SERIES B. ARCIFERA.

3. BUFONIDÆ.

Synopsis of Genera.

Fingers and toes more or less webbed, the tips dilated into regular discs; sternum cartilaginous. 1. Nectophryne, p. 44.

Fingers free, toes more or less webbed; sternum either cartilaginous, or with a semi-ossified style. 2. Bufo, p. 44.

1. NECTOPHRYNE.

1. NECTOPHRYNE TUBERCULOSA [PLATE XI. 1. A.B.].

Nectophryne tuberculosa, *Blgr. Cat.* 1882, p. 280.
Pedostibes tuberculosus, *Günth. Proc. Zool. Soc.* 1875, p. 576, pl. LXIV, fig. C.

Habit moderately slender; snout sub-acuminate; tympanum distinct, one-third the width of the eye; fingers webbed at the base; toes nearly entirely webbed; tips of fingers and toes dilated into broad truncated discs, those of the toes rather smaller than those of the fingers; two small, flat metatarsal tubercles. Skin of the upper parts tubercular, the largest tubercles being arranged along each side of the back. Colour and markings (of spirit specimens): brownish grey above, sides darker; a white band from below the eye to the axil; another white longitudinal band in the lumbar region; beneath dark spotted.

Specimens in the British Museum from Malabar.

2. BUFO.

Synopsis of Species.

A. *Crown without bony ridges.*

1. First finger shorter than second; toes more than half-webbed; no parotoids. 1. *pulcher*, p. 45.

2. First finger as long as or longer than second.

a. Parotoids distinct; tympanum nearly as large as the eye; no tarsal fold; skin smooth. 2. *hololius*, p. 45.

b. Parotoids distinct; tympanum very small; toes nearly entirely webbed; no tarsal fold; sub-articular tubercles of toes simple; snout projecting. 3. *beddomii*, p. 45.

B. *Crown with bony ridges.*

1. No parietal ridges ; orbito-tympanic ridges not much developed.

Cranial ridges very distinct ; tympanum at least two-thirds the width of the eye.   4. *melanostictus*, p. 46.

Cranial ridges very distinct ; tympanum very small.

5. *microtympanum*, p. 47.

2. A parietal ridge.

Supero-orbital and parietal ridges forming an angle together; tympanum two-thirds the width of the eye ; tarso-metatarsal articulation not reaching beyond the tip of the snout, when the leg is drawn forwards.

6. *parietalis*, p. 47.

1. BUFO PULCHER [PLATE XI. 2].

Bufo pulcher, *Blgr. Cat.* 1882, p. 288.
Ansonia ornata, *Günth. Proc. Zool. Soc.* 1875, p. 568, pl. LXIII, fig. A.

Habit slender; crown without bony ridges; tympanum distinct, about half the size of the eye; first finger much shorter than second ; toes nearly entirely webbed; tips of fingers and toes slightly swollen ; two metatarsal tubercles. Anterior half of the back finely tubercular, the remainder smooth ; no parotoids. Colour and markings (of spirit specimens): black; upper side of the head and a dorsal line grey ; beneath with large bright yellow spots.

Specimens in the British Museum from the Brumagherris.

2. BUFO HOLOLIUS [PLATE XI. 3].

Bufo hololius, *Günth. Proc. Zool. Soc.* 1875, p. 569, pl. LXIV, fig. A.; *Blgr. Cat.* 1882, p. 289.

Crown without bony ridges ; tympanum very distinct, nearly as large as the eye; first finger extending a little beyond the second ; toes webbed at the base only ; two small metatarsal tubercles. Skin smooth, the back with very flat, smooth, distinctly porous, glandular patches ; parotoid flat, distinct. Colour and markings (of spirit specimens) : upper parts olive coloured, marbled with brown; lower parts whitish.

A single specimen in the British Museum from Malabar.

3. BUFO BEDDOMII [PLATE XI. 4].

Bufo beddomii, *Günth. Proc. Zool. Soc.* 1875, p. 569; *Blgr. Cat.* 1882, p. 289, pl. XIX, fig. 1.
Bufo travancoricus, *Bedd. Proc. Zool. Soc.* 1877, p. 685.

Crown without bony ridges ; tympanum very small, sometimes indistinct ; first finger not extending beyond second; toes nearly entirely webbed ; two small metatarsal tubercles. Upper parts covered with rough tubercles ; parotoids ovate, about twice as long as broad, rather indistinct. Colour and markings (of spirit specimens): above dark brown, with some indistinct black spots ; limbs beautifully marbled with carmine ; lower surfaces marbled with brown.

Specimens in the British Museum from Malabar and the Chokam Patty hills (4,000 feet). A single specimen was captured, under an old rotten log, in dense moist forest, above the Ayencoil pass (Travancore), at about 2,500 feet elevation, by Colonel Beddome, who describes (*l.c. Bufo travancoricus*) its colour as " blackish brown ; the thighs, arms, and legs beautifully marbled with carmine ; the tubercles of the body often tipped with the same colour ; those of the belly often whitish."

4. BUFO MELANOSTICTUS [PLATE XII. 1].

Bufo melanostictus, *Schneid. Hist. Amph.* p. 216; *Gravenh, Delic.* p. 57; *Cantor. Cat. Mal. Rept.* p. 142; *Girard. U. S. Expl. Exped. Herp.* p. 92, pl. V, figs. 10–14; *Günth. Cat.* 1858, p. 61, and *Rept. Brit. Ind.* p. 422; *Steindachn, Novara. Amph.* p. 42; *Stoliczka, Proc. As. Soc. Beng.* 1870, p. 155; *Blgr. Cat.* 1882, p. 306.

Bufo scaber, *Daud. Rain.* p. 94, pl. 34, fig. 1, and *Rept.* VIII, p. 194; *Tschudi., Batr.* p. 88; *Dum. & Bibr.* p. 699; *Schleg. Abbild.* p. 64, pl. 20, fig. 2.

Bufo bengalensis, *Daud. Rain.* p. 96, pl. 35, fig. 1, and *Rept.* VIII, p. 197; *Lesson in Bélang. Voy. Ind. Or. Rept.* p. 334.

Bufo isos, *Günth. Cat.* 1858, p. 62; *Lesson, l.c.* p. 333, pl. 7 ; *Dum. & Bibr.* p. 702.

Bufo dubia (*Shaw*) *Gray. Ind. Zool.*

Bufo carinatus, *Gray. l.c.,*

Bufo gymnauchen, *Bleeker, Nat. Tijdschr. Nederl. Ind.* 1858, XVI, p. 46.

Phrynoidis melanostictus, *Cope. Proc. Ac. Philad.* 1863, p. 357.

Bufo spinipes (*Fitzing*) *Steindachn. l.c.* p. 43, pl. 5, fig. 6.

Head with more or less elevated bony ridges ; tympanum at least two-thirds the width of the eye ; first finger generally extending beyond second ; toes at least half-webbed ; two moderate metatarsal tubercles. Upper surfaces with more or less prominent, generally spiny warts ; parotoids very prominent, kidney shaped or elliptic, more or less elongate. Colour and markings (of spirit specimens): yellowish or brownish above, the spines of the warts and the ridges of the head generally black ; beneath immaculate or more or less spotted.

This species, the commonest toad in Southern India, is, says Günther (*Rept. Brit. Ind.*, p. 422), "one of the most common Batrachians of the Indian region, and appears to inhabit every part of the continent and of the Archipelago, from the peninsula of the Southern India to China and the Philippine Islands ; in the Himalayas it ascends to an altitude of 9,000 feet." In Southern India it is found at all levels from the plains up to 7,000 feet. It makes a characteristic chirping sound, and sometimes emits a shrill whistle. The length of the full grown animal is subject to great variations, and, whereas a typical specimen in the Madras Museum from Madras measures only 4¾ inches from the tip of the snout to the tip of the longest toe, a specimen from Cochin measures as much as 5¾ inches between the same points.

A specimen of a full grown male in the Madras Museum shows the fore-limb swollen for breeding purposes. The young, which are very abundant in Madras during the November monsoon, go through their tadpole stage in water.

Specimens in the British Museum from Madras; in the Madras Museum from Madras, Cochin, Ootacamund and Kotagiri (6,000 feet).

Many of the specimens, which I have examined on the Nilgiris, in the neighbourhood of Coonoor and Kotagiri, where this species is very abundant in damp places, and the banks of streams, are very much larger than any which I have seen in the plains, and the females are far larger than the males. The measurements of the largest female, (captured during the breeding season) which I have seen, are length of body 3½ inches, hind leg 4 inches. Some of the Nilgiri specimens had, during life, bright red markings, or a diffuse red staining on the upper surface of the body, while the colour of others was a uniform pale yellow.

5. BUFO MICROTYMPANUM [PLATE XIII. 1].

Bufo microtympanum, *Blgr. Cat.* 1882, p. 307, pl. XXII, fig. 1.

Head with prominent bony ridges; tympanum very small, not half the width of the eye; first finger extending beyond second; toes about half-webbed; two metatarsal tubercles. Upper surfaces with irregular, distinctly porous warts; parotoids prominent, elliptic, twice or twice and-a-half longer than broad. Colour and markings (of spirit specimens) : dark brown above, yellow beneath, marbled with brown.

Specimens in the British Museum from Malabar; in the Madras Museum from Kodaikánal, Pulney hills (7,000 feet). I have also seen it on the Nilgiris, in a hole in decayed wood in a forest near Coonoor.

6. BUFO PARIETALIS [PLATE XIII, 2].

Bufo parietalis, *Blgr. Cat.* 1882, p. 312, pl. XXI, fig. 2.

Crown with very prominent ridges; tympanum two-thirds the width of the eye; first finger extending beyond second; toes half webbed; two metatarsal tubercles. Upper surfaces covered with irregular warts; parotoids elliptic, very prominent. Colour and markings (of spirit specimens) : uniform brown above; beneath marbled with brown.

Specimens in the British Museum from Malabar.

ORDER II. APODA.

No limbs; tail rudimentary. Males with an intromittent copulatory organ. Adapted for burrowing.

FAMILY. CŒCILIIDÆ.

Synopsis of Genera.

Cycloid imbricated scales imbedded in the skin, at least on the borders of the circular folds ; eyes distinct.

Tentacle conical, exsertile, surrounded by a ring-shaped groove, situated between the nostril and the eye, near the lip.

1. Ichthyophis, p. 48.

Tentacle as in the preceding, but situated below the nostril.

2. Uræotyphlus, p. 49.

1. ICHTHYOPHIS.[1]

1. ICHTHYOPHIS GLUTINOSUS.

Ichthyophis glutinosus, *Gray. Cat.* 1850, p. 60; *Peters, Mon. Berl. Ac.* 1879, p. 931, pl. figs. 1–4; *Blgr. Cat.* 1882, p. 89, pl. IV, fig. 2.

Rhinatrema bivittatum, *Gray. Cat.* p. 61.

Serpens cœcilia ceylonica, *Seba*, ii. p. 26, tab. 25, fig. 2.

Cœcilia glutinosa, *Linn. Mus. Ad. Fred.* p. 19, pl. XXV, fig. 2, and *S. N. i*, p. 229; *Daud. Rept.* VII, p. 418; *Peters, Mon. Berl. Ac.* 1864, p. 303.

Cœcilia viscosa, *Latr. Rept.* IV, p. 238.

Ichthyophis hasseltii, *Fitzing. Neue. Classif. Rept.* p. 63.

Cœcilia hypocyanea, *Hasselt. Isis.* 1827, p. 565; *Müller, Zeitschr. f. Phys.* IV., p. 195, and *Arch. Anat. Phys.* 1835, p. 391, pl. 8, figs. 12–14; *Schleg. Abbild.* p. 119, pl. 3?, fig. 1.

Cœcilia bivittata, *Cuv. R. A.* 2nd ed. ii, p. 100.

Epicrium hypocyanea, *Wagl. Syst. Amph.* p. 198; *Tschudi. Batr.* p. 90.

Epicrium glutinosum, *Dum. & Bibr.* p. 286; *Günth. Rept. Brit. Ind.* 1864, p. 441.

Rhinatrema bivittatum, *Dum. & Bibr.* p. 288, pl. 85, fig. 4.

Ichthyophis beddomii, *Peters, l.c.* p. 932, pl. fig. 4.

Both rows of mandibular teeth well developed; snout rounded; width of head between the eyes equals the distance of the eye from the end of the snout; eye easily distinguishable; tentacle below and in front of the eye, generally much nearer the eye than the nostril. Body sub-cylindrical, rather depressed, moderately elongate, with very numerous (240 to 400) distinct circular folds, angular on the belly. Tail very short though distinct, pointed. Dark brown or bluish black; a yellow band along each side of the body, from the head to the tail.

In the larva of this species, says Boulenger (*l.c.*), " the head is fish-like, greatly resembling that of *Amphiuma*, provided with much developed labial lobes; the tongue is extensively free in front. The tentacle-pit is either absent or close to the eye. The latter is much more developed than in the adult, about as much as in the *Amphiumidæ*. I cannot find any branchiæ. The spiracula are large. The tail is much more distinct than in the adult, strongly compressed, and finned above and beneath, the upper membrane extending somewhat in advance of the vent. The circular folds are very indistinct in the youngest specimens, becoming gradually more distinct as the animal grows. The anal opening is a longitudinal cleft."

According to P. B. and C. F. Sarasin, this species (called *Epicrium glutinosum*) is oviparous. The eggs are very similar to those of

---

[1] A species, *Epicrium carnosum*, not recorded in the British Museum Catalogue, is described by Colonel Beddome (*Madras. Month. Journ. Med. Sc.*, II, 1870, p. 176) as found under stones on the Peria Peek, Wynaad, at an elevation of about 5,000 feet, of which the following are some of the characteristics: " Head very much depressed; eyes quite invisible; labial groove much nearer the nasal than the eye; point of tail quite rounded, not prolonged more than half a line or a line beyond the vent; annular folds 126, quite continued round the body and belly throughout the whole length; total length seven inches with a circumference about as thick as a crow's quill: of a uniform bright fleshy colour when alive, fading to a reddish brown in spirit."

Sauropsida: they are exceptionally large (9 mm. long), of an oval shape, and possess a large yolk, which is light yellow in colour, and consists of both yellow and white granules. They are coated with a tough albumen in the oviduct, and this becomes drawn out at the poles into chalazæ, by means of which the eggs are connected together like the beads of a necklace. They are laid in the earth, and the mother coils herself round them.

Specimens in the British Museum from the Wynaad and the Nílgiris; in the Madras Museum from the Wynaad: length 7¼ inches.

2. ICHTHYOPHIS MONOCHROUS.

Ichthyophis monochrous, *Peters, Mon. Berl. Ac.* 1879, p. 932 ; *Blgr. Cat.* 1882, p. 91, pl. IV, fig. 1.

Epicrium monochroum, *Bleeker. Nat. Tydschr. Nederl. Ind.* XVI. 1858, p. 188 ; *Günth. Rept. Brit. Ind.* 1864, p. 443.

Head shorter than that of the preceding ; the distance between the eyes more than the length of the snout ; inner series of mandibular teeth indistinct, composed of a few teeth only. 235 to 360 circular folds. Uniform blackish-brown or lead-coloured, without lateral band. Total length 330 mm.

Specimens in the British Museum from Malabar.

2. URÆOTYPHLUS.

1. URÆOTYPHLUS OXYURUS.

Uræotyphlus oxyurus, *Peters, Mon. Berl. Ac.* 1879, p. 933; and *Sitzb. Ges. Nat. Fr.* 1881, p. 90; *Blgr. Cat.* 1882, p. 92, pl. V, fig. 2.

Cœcilia oxyura, *Gray. Cat.* 1850, p. 58 ; *Dum. & Bibr.* p. 280 ; *A. Dum. l.c.* p. 22, pl. 1, fig. 8 ; *Günth. Rept. Brit. Ind.* 1864, p. 443.

Teeth small, subequal ; both rows of mandibular teeth well developed ; snout narrow, rounded ; width of the head between the eyes equals the distance of the eye from the tip of the snout ; tentacle small, below the nostril, close to the lip; eyes easily distinguishable. Body cylindrical, moderately elongate, with numerous (200 to 210) distinct circular folds, widely interrupted on the belly (except those on the hindermost part of the body), alternately longer and shorter. Tail very short, though distinct, pointed. Blackish or purplish-brown, lighter parts (sometime white) beneath ; lips and folds on the sides light. Total length 280 mm.

Specimens in the British Museum from the Anamallays, Malabar, and Tinnevelly ; in the Madras Museum from Malabar : length 8¼ inches.

2. URÆOTYPHLUS MALABARICUS.

Uræotyphlus malabaricus, *Peters, Mon. Berl. Ac.* 1879, p. 933 ; *Blgr. Cat.* 1882, p. 92, pl. V, fig. 3.

Cœcilia malabarica, *Bedd. Madras Month. Journ. Med. Sc.* ii. 1870, p. 170.

Snout narrow and more prominent than that of the preceding, measuring more than the distance between the eyes ; folds more numerous

(240 to 260), interrupted on the belly by a very narrow interspace. Dark olive-brown, a little lighter beneath; lips and end of snout yellowish. Total length 230 mm. The characters of this species are described by Colonel Beddome (*l.c.*) as : " Body short, total length 5½ inches, as thick as a goose's quill, terminating in a pointed tail, which is prolonged to about one-seventh of an inch beyond the vent ; body and tail surrounded by 238 folds, almost every one of which meet under the belly ; snout flattened and shelving downwards, sub-nasal grooves at the edge of the flattened snout below, but rather in front of the nasals.

Malabar, rare, a much smaller species than the common *C. oxyura*, and differing in its snout and the annular rings."

Specimens in the British Museum from Malabar.

ALPHABETICAL INDEX.

ADDENDA.

LIST OF PLATES.

Plate I.

Skeleton of *Rana hexadactyla.*

Fig. 1. Bony skull viewed from above.
" 2. Bony skull viewed from beneath.
" 3. Mandible.
" 4. Vertebral column and urostyle.
" 5. Left half of pelvic girdle.

Plate II.

Skeleton of *Rana hexadactyla.*

Fig. 1. Femur.
" 2. United tibia and fibula and tarsus.
" 3. Metatarsus and phalanges.
" 4. Pectoral girdle.
" 5. Bones of anterior extremity (humerus, united radius and ulna, carpus, metacarpus, and phalanges.)

Plate III.

Rana hexadactyla, Less.

Plate IV.

Fig. 1. *Rana cyanophlyctis*, Schn. (after *Günther*, *P. Z. S.* 1867, pl. XXVIII, fig. B.)
" 2. *Rana verrucosa*, Günth. (after *Blgr. Cat.* 1882, pl. IV, fig. 1.)
" 3. *Rana breviceps*, Schn. (after *Günther*, *Cat.* 1858, pl. II, fig. A.)
" 4. *Rana dobsonii*, Blgr. (after *Blgr. Cat.* 1882, pl. III, fig. 1.)

Plate V.

Fig. 1. A. B. *Rana beddomii*, Günth. (after *Günther*, *P. Z. S.* 1875, pl. LXIII, fig. B.)
" 2. *Rana semipalmata*, Blgr. (after *Blgr. Cat.* 1882, pl. IV, fig. 3.)
" 3. *Rana diplosticta*, Günth. (after *Günther*, *P. Z. S.* 1875, pl. LXIII, fig. C.)
" 4. *Rana temporalis*, Günth. (after *Günther*, *Rept. Brit. Ind.* 1864, pl. XXVI, fig. G.)

Plate VI.

Fig. 1. *Rhacophorus pleurostictus*, Günth. (after *Günther*, *Rept. Brit. Ind.* 1864, pl. XXVI, fig. 1.)
" 2. A. B. *Ixalus opisthorhodus*, Günth. (after *Günther*, *P. Z. S.* 1868, pl. XXXVII, figs. 3 and 3*a*).

Fig. 3. *Izalus leucorhinus*, Mart. (after *Günther, Rept. Brit. Ind.* 1864, pl. XXVI, fig. E.)
,, 4. *Izalus femoralis*, Günth. (after *Günther, Rept. Brit. Ind.* 1864, pl. XXVI, fig. D.)
,, 5. *Izalus fuscus*, Blgr. (after *Blgr. Cat.* 1882, pl. X, fig. 3.)

PLATE VII.

Fig. 1. *Izalus beddomii*, Günth. (after *Blgr. Cat.* 1882, pl. X, fig. 7.)
,, 2. *Izalus variabilis*, Günth. (after *Günther, Cat.* 1858, pl. IV, fig. A.)
,, 3. *Izalus glandulosus*, Jerd. (after *Günther, P. Z. S.* 1875, pl. LXVI, fig. A.)
,, 4. *Izalus chalazodes*, Günth. (after *Günther, P. Z. S.* 1875, pl. LXVI, fig. B.)
,, 5. *Izalus flaviventris*, Blgr. (after *Blgr. Cat.* 1882, pl. XI, fig. 1.)
,, 6. *Izalus signatus*, Blgr. (after *Blgr. Cat.* 1882, pl. XI, fig. 2.)

PLATE VIII.

Fig. 1. *Nyctibatrachus pygmæus*, Günth. (after *Blgr. Cat.* 1882, pl. XII, fig. 1.)
,, 2. *Nyctibatrachus major*, Blgr. (after *Blgr. Cat.* 1882, pl. XII, fig. 2.)
,, 3. *Callula obscura*, Günth. (after *Blgr. Cat.* 1882, pl. XIII, fig. 3.)
,, 4. *Callula obscura*, Günth. (after *Günther, P. Z. S.* 1875, pl. LXIV, fig. B.)
,, 5. *Callula triangularis*, Günth. (after *Blgr. Cat.* 1882, pl. XIII, fig. 4.)

PLATE IX.

Cacopus systoma, Schn.

PLATE X.

Cacopus globulosus, Günth.

PLATE XI.

Fig. 1. A. B. *Nectophryne tuberculosa*, Günth. (after *Günther, P. Z. S.* 1875, pl. LXIV, fig. C.)
,, 2. *Bufo pulcher*, Blgr. (after *Günther, P. Z. S.* 1875, pl. LXIII, fig. A.)
,, 3. *Bufo hololius*, Günth. (after *Günther, P. Z. S.* 1875, pl. LXIV, fig. A.)
,, 4. *Bufo beddomii*, Günth. (after *Blgr. Cat.* 1882, pl. XXI, fig. 1.)

PLATE XII.

Bufo melanostictus, Schn.

PLATE XIII.

Fig. 1. *Bufo microtympanum*, Blgr. (after *Blgr. Cat.* 1882, pl. XXII, fig. 1.)
,, 2. *Bufo parietalis*, Blgr. (after *Blgr. Cat.* 1882, pl. XXI, fig. 2.)

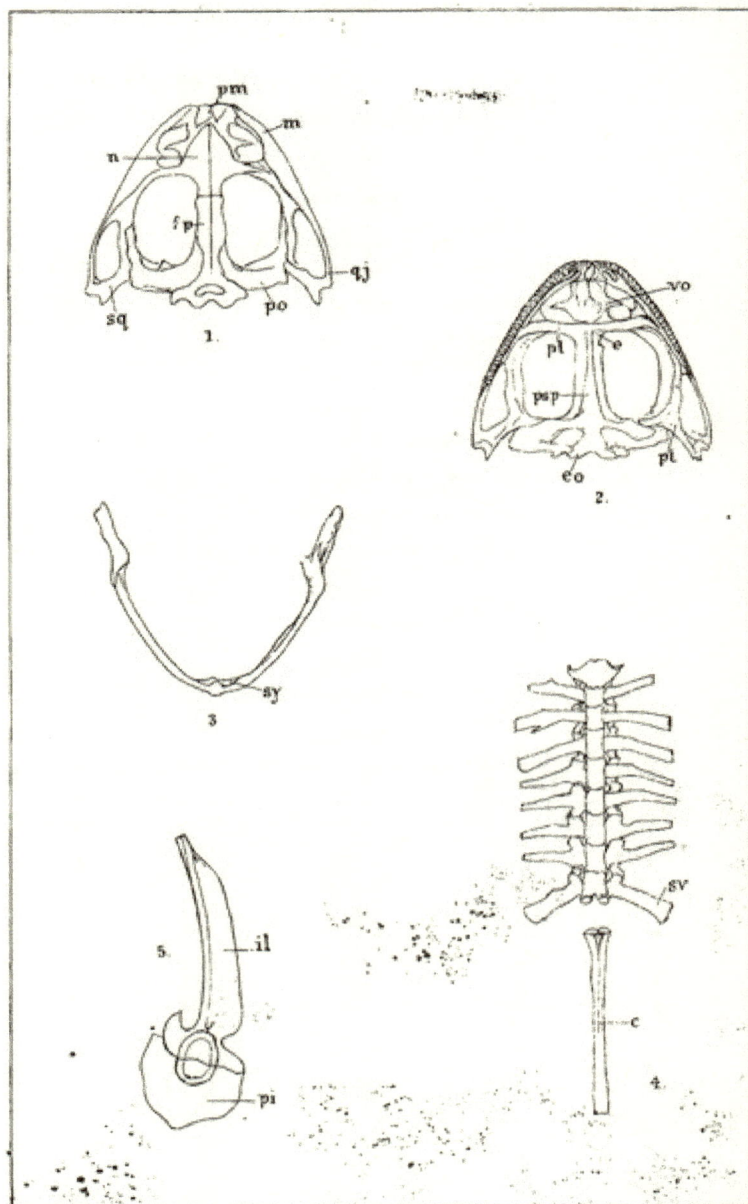

SKELETON OF RANA HEXADACTYLA

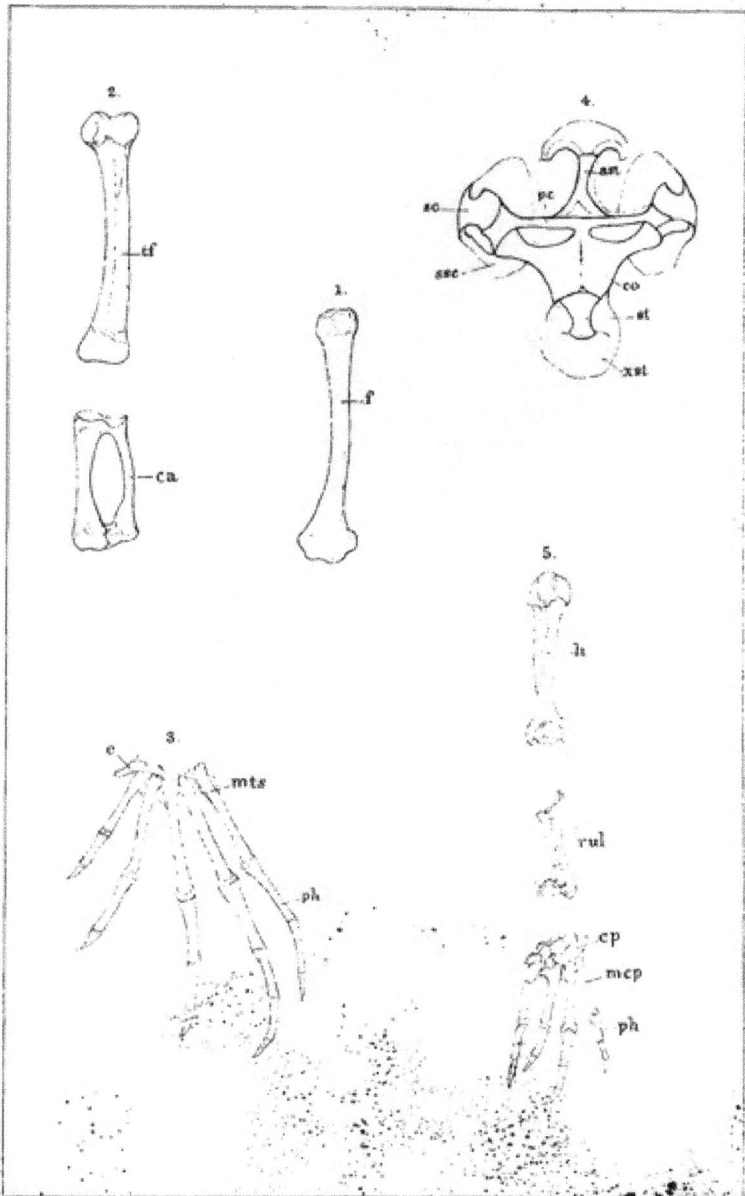

SKELETON OF RANA HEXADACTYLA

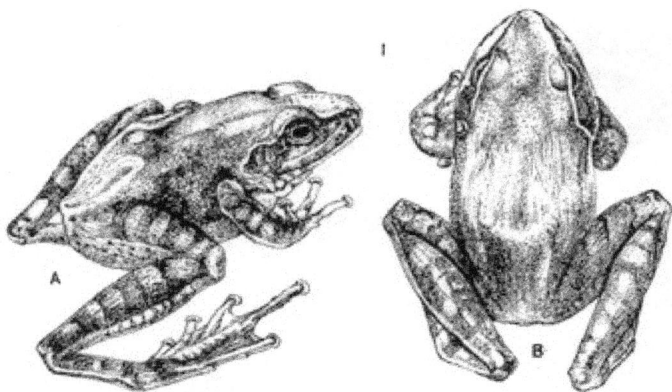

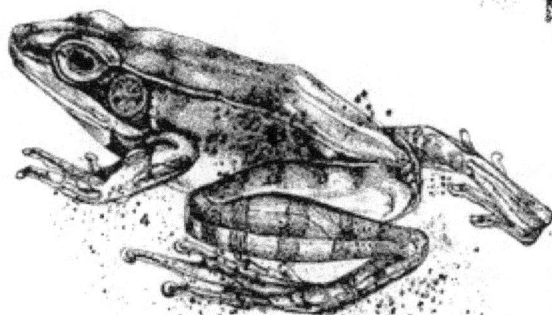

1. A.B. RANA BEDDOMII. 2. RANA SEMIPALMATA.
3. RANA DIPLOSTICTA. 4. RANA TEMPORALIS.

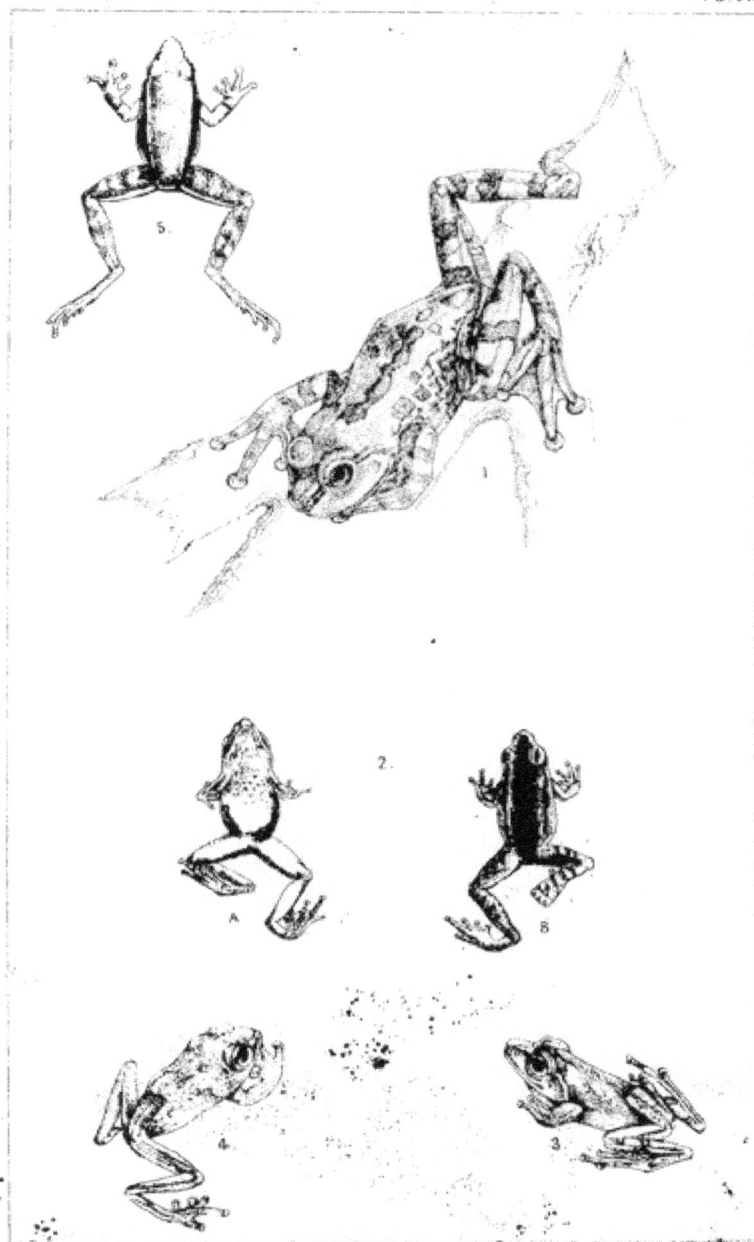

1. RHACOPHORUS PLEUROSTICTUS. A. B. IXALUS OPISTHORHODUS.
3. IXALUS LEUCORHINUS. 4. IXALUS FEMORALIS. 5 IXALUS FUSCUS.

1. IXALUS BEDDOMII.   2.IXALUS VARIABILIS.
3. IXALUS GLANDULOSUS, 4.IXALUS CHALAZODES.
5. IXALUS FLAVIVENTRIS. 6. IXALUS SIGNATUS.

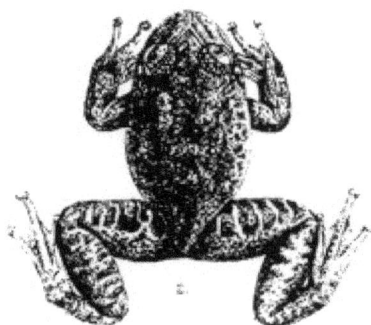

1. BATRACHUS PYGMAEUS. 2. NYCTIMYSTES MAJOR.
3. RANA OLIVACEA. 4. RAPELLA TRIANGULARIS.

1.

I.

CACOPUS GLOBULOSUS

1. A.B. NECTOPHRYNE TUBERCULOSA. 2. BUFO PULCHER
3. BUFO HOLOLIUS 4. BUFO BEDDOMII

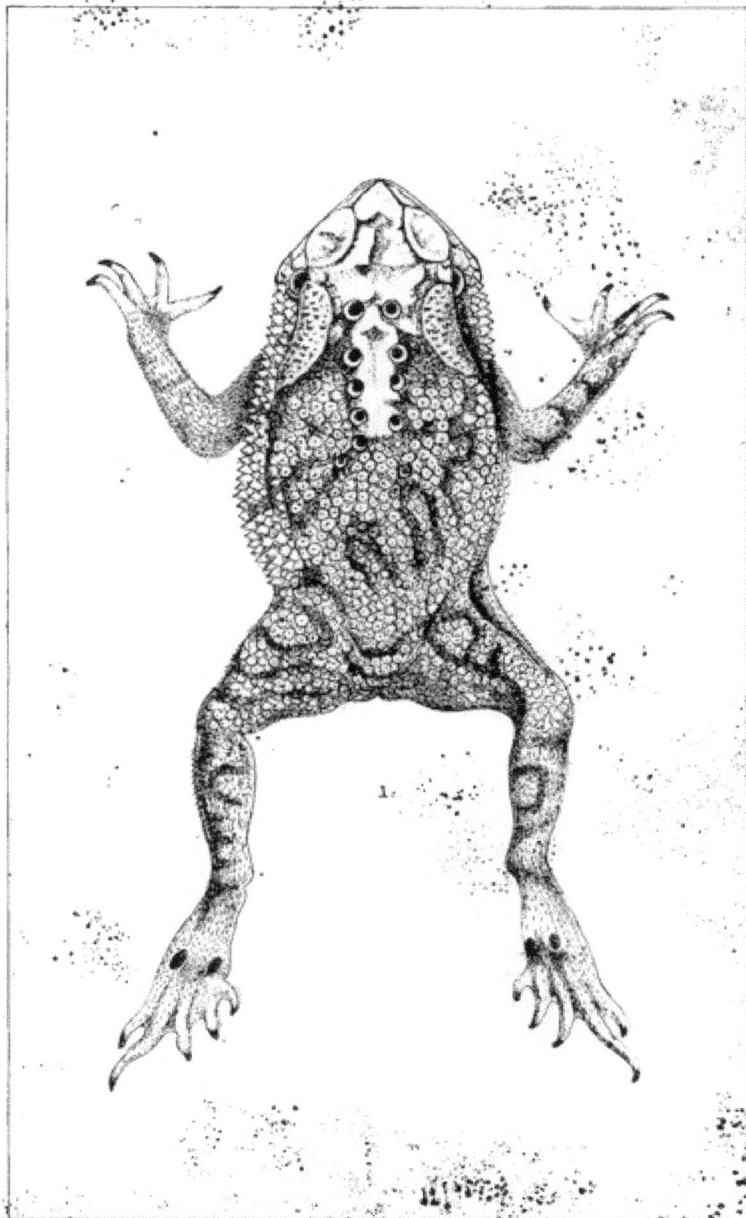

ALEX. BARREN LITHOG. MADRAS. 1887

BUFO MELANOSTICTUS.

1 BUFO MICROTYMPANUM. 2 BUFO PARIETALIS.

www.ingramcontent.com/pod-product-compliance
Lightning Source LLC
Chambersburg PA
CBHW022026080426
42733CB00007B/745